Sharing the kno

Copyright © 2013 Alex Polyakov

ISBN: 978-0-9852884-1-9

Published by Table Tennis Achievements Publishing

Book Cover by Zoran Stefanovski

All rights reserved, including the right to reproduce this work, in whole or in part, in any form.

To my daughter Alyssa, your eager learning from the very first days you were born inspired me to share the knowledge with others. May you always enjoy learning and discovering new things the same way you do now.

The Next Step

by

Alex Polyakov

Table of Contents

Preface 9
Prerequisite 11
   Beyond the Strokes 13
   Reading the Game 21
   Action, Reaction 29
   The Best Technique 36
   Control 44
   Power and Control 55
   Spin and Speed 59
   The Next Step of Development 63

Strategy and Tactics 67
Strategy 69
   Strategic Planning 72
   The Opening 79
   Types of Strategy 82
   Strategic Approach 88
   The Middle Game 95
   The End Game 98
   Innovation 102
   Developing Strategic Sense 105

Tactics 109
   Tactical Awareness 112
   Principles of Tactics 114

Tactical Approach	117
Tactical Geometry	126
Placement	137
Tactical Dimensions	146
The Pin and a Switch	149
Development of Tactics	159
The Mental Game	*162*
Mental Basics	165
Attitude	169
Concentration	176
Failure	186
Being a champion	193
Talent	197
Intervention	201
Knowing self	213
The Next Step	*223*
Conclusion	*230*
Contributors	*232*
References	*233*

Preface

"The more I live, the more I learn. The more I learn, the more I realize, the less I know."
- Michel Legrand

Since the publication of my previous book "Breaking 2000", I have spent many hours thinking about the next book. There has been a lot of feedback from many readers. Most of the feedback was positive which inspired me to take the next step - bringing this book to life and hence the title of this book.

There are a lot of players of various levels. My quest to improve to a higher level of the game is what prompted me to continue documenting my thoughts. Why are better players so good? What makes them so special? Why do some players improve and others do not? Why do some players improve quicker and some go through a long and grueling challenge? What do I need to know to realize the full potential of my abilities? Where are the pitfalls of high level players and how can I avoid making the same mistakes?

In short, this book is about table tennis, but in this book, I will dive deeper within the foundation of the game, and the very elements that separate the great players from the good players. This is not a book for a beginner that will allow one to learn the strokes. This is also not a book on how to train. This is also not a book about me. This book will provide detailed insights on four essential parts of the game - technique, strategy, tactics, and the mental game. This is a reference material based on a relentless pursuit to understand many other dimensions of the game that are vital for player's next step onto higher levels.

The aim of this book is to create a different type of an artifact and go beyond the same basics documented in many ways by many players and coaches. The goal is to describe numerous principles of table tennis and to show how to apply vast amount of table tennis knowledge to construct player's most effective game using the skills that the player has already mastered as well as to describe many other skills of the game that the player may choose to develop.

Every player reading the same pages of the book will pick up different things depending on the player's past experiences. What one will find valuable, new, and insightful another might find to be a repeat. Yet, the book is written in such a way to build various concepts as if they are puzzles of a much bigger picture attached in a very particular way. I am certain that every player will appreciate not only the new pictures that will be created with every puzzle put together after reading the book, but also the way many puzzles relate and interweave with each other, and how they draw out an even larger picture. The bigger picture again, being a roadmap to further improvement.

With these words, I would like to thank all the wonderful individuals that have contributed to my growth as a player, writer, and an athlete - Gerald Reid, Alex (Fangyi) Liu, Mika Bey, Ronnie Cruz, and Ilya Ovrutsky.

Prerequisite

> "The more technique you have, the less you have to worry about it. The more technique there is, the less there is."
> - Pablo Picasso

Michel Gadal, National Coach for France and Canada who is famed for coaching and mentoring Jean-Philippe Gatien on his way to become a World Champion and an Olympic Silver Medalist, the greatest French table tennis player of all time, has said in his book "Train to Win", "learning how to play, is in my opinion a much more important level than learning technique." I strongly agree with this statement.

Look into your match history, or any other player that you know dearly for that matter. I am certain you will find a match that was won against a much better player, a player who is considered to be so good that he undoubtedly possesses all the elements of technique necessary to win. Are such upsets common? Maybe not too common, but the upsets occur quite often even at the world class level.

Why? It's not luck, even if the match is won with a net or an edge ball in the final point because to get to that victorious scenario, the lower ranked player had to win a few games, maintaining his best performance throughout the match, keeping up in close games, decreasing point deficits and taking leads. The victory is possible because technique that stands on its own does not guarantee to produce a victory. A strong technical foundation is simply not enough to win. One needs to know how to *properly* apply the technique.

Technique is the approach, it is the fundamental knowledge, and it is the core. Technique is what will allow the player to execute a desired shot with success when needed, but it is not a formula for success. It is just one single variable from many others that exist during the match. Techniques are specific tangible skills, but the result of the match will not directly depend on techniques. It will depend on the player's approach to the match and the ability to quickly find proper solutions to various problems occurring in the points.

This section of the book describes many principles of this approach. It is a very important pre-requisite of the other chapters. The concepts contained herein are like glue used to bond multiple vital elements of the game together. They are fundamentals necessary to draft a plan for improvement.

Beyond the Strokes

If you were to close your eyes and think of strokes, what will you see? I will take a stab at it by guessing your answer to this question. You see yourself warming up with a forehand loop. Why? It is the main shot in table tennis. It is not a surprise to me that most people see exactly that. Strokes are synonymous with the action of simply hitting the ball, but by itself this action has no association to the game, especially at the higher level.

At the beginner and intermediate levels, many players put too much emphasis on a continuous development of the strokes, especially in isolation from the real environment where the strokes will need to be applied. The ever changing dynamic nature of table tennis demands more than a stroke. It demands a set of strokes in various environments - positional, spin oriented, speed oriented, time constrained, and mentally pressured. This is one of the reasons why improvement in table tennis becomes exponentially more difficult as the skill level progresses higher. The players must acquire a significant amount of experience in order to learn to deal with certain scenarios and learn to apply proper strokes to the ever changing situation on the court.

Interestingly enough, when most players think about strokes, they do not think of technique. What is technique? Technique is *how* you execute the stroke. It is difficult to describe technique in table tennis because of so many various elements that technique consists of. For example, against a specific type of a shot, where do you ideally place your feet to return the ball? How wide? How far do you bend your knees? How far should be the backswing? How much do you open or close the paddle for the incoming spin? Do you apply wrist for extra touch or spin? How fast do you swing? Where to do you follow through to end the stroke? How far do you rotate your body? How do you recover to prepare for the next shot?

This is only a brief list of check points. Lots more questions can be spawned from the answers to the abovementioned questions to draw out more details of a specific technique. Unfortunately during the rally, there is no time to ask these questions. Nor is there time to come up with the answers. The game is too fast for that.

Table tennis players do not have the luxury to stop during the rally and think about all the elements of technique that go into a stroke - we must be capable of recognizing incoming shots early and responding to them. Our responses should not be rash or desperate reactions. They should be smooth and almost gracious movements that adhere to the principles of proper technique. If at least one element of technique is not executed properly, the chance of an unforced error increases drastically. Yet, the only time when all of the elements of technique can be flawlessly executed is in practice. It is achieved by creating a stable environment when a training partner focuses on returning the ball *to* you as a collaborator instead of away from you as a competitor.

Entering a typical table tennis club, we see players practice in controlled environments without the dynamics that exist in real matches. Forehand to forehand counter hitting for example is a most common way players practice. When asked what the players are working on, their response is "strokes." These players, however, are benefiting very little from the training routine they have created. Over time, the only thing you begin to notice is the players beginning to hit the ball harder. Yet, the purpose of the training begins to fade away. The improvement initially gained by this training routine over time becomes less and less productive to the overall development and maturity of a player. This is exactly why forehand to forehand, backhand to backhand, and forehand to backhand training is considered to be more of a warm up rather than a practice routine. Certainly for a very beginner this type of training is necessary to learn the proper technique, but once the technique becomes repeatable with good consistency, it is time to take the next step forward - it is time to look beyond the strokes.

In my teens, my friends began to get involved in martial arts. My parents luckily allowed me to follow my friends and train at a local dojo called Karate Club Olympic. Our sensei had a complete curriculum for all of his students, but we had a lot more energy. We were inspired by the movies full of martial arts heroes and trained things that were border line stunts instead of actual skills the discipline was teaching us. One day, we were training in the dojo before the class, while our sensei was in his office. One girl's father, also an accomplished martial artist, stopped by the club to watch our class train that day. We were preparing for competition and he wanted to see what we were up to and how our training was progressing. After the training, he came over and said: "You are all good at many things, but to win in a tournament, you need to be great at only one thing, but know how to set it up, and be prepared to strike."

He really impressed us with his thoughts because he was completely right. Each and every one of us had a special skill we did better than another, but we have not recognized its significance until that day. During sparring we attempted all kinds of wild combinations that looked good, but never produced significant results. Until that moment, we did not aim to use our strengths. Most of us did not even know what our real strengths were!

The same holds true in table tennis - more emphasis needs to be put towards customizing a player's game to player's strengths. This is exactly what makes the difference between winning and participating. A player who knows the strengths and weaknesses of his game is aware how he must approach the game in order to win. The player that does not know himself keeps probing the opponent with different shots, while the result remains largely uncertain.

Looking at the game using the "know thyself" principle, mere strokes begin to lose much of their prior importance. The player now does not need to be concerned with raising consistency on the strokes he will likely never use in the game and can certainly make his training significantly more efficient by working on shots that will be applicable to the type of the game the player prefers to play.

High level players are not concerned with strokes and the reason for it is simple - to improve and compete at a high level, the player must have already mastered majority of the strokes that allowed the player to advance to a higher level. The fact of the matter is that players at many levels have certain shots that allow them to win points outright even against better players.

Therefore, it is not the stroke that wins the point, game, or match. It is the *application* of the stroke in the game. What makes the biggest difference is *how* the player is able to set up a point winning shot. Being able to set up the point winning shot in order to execute your best shot against opponent's weakness is what makes a very intelligent table tennis player. This player, even if he only has one killer shot, but is able to set it up on a consistent basis, becomes a much tougher adversary.

Combination training is the next requirement for an improving player, once the knowledge of the stroke is sound and the execution is pretty good. Why is pretty good stroke execution instead of perfect execution enough to move to the next stage? Perfecting shot's execution in a controlled environment is good for a personal gratification, but the return on the investment by training to perfection will be minimal. At this point, it is best to increase the difficulty of the training routine by creating an environment that will mimic a competitive match. All it takes is adding a service, service return, or a random placement element somewhere in a routine. Hence, learning to consistently set up a strong shot in the game now becomes much more important and beneficial.

Combination training is aimed to improve a delivery of a sequence of shots. This type of training simulates an exchange of shots during a real match. At the initial stages, this training uses very basic common patterns, but at a higher level, the aim is to reproduce the very sequences that led up to a point loss. This type of an approach to dissect the point allows zeroing in on a mistake in fine detail. Was it a problem with technique? A tactical mistake? A timing mistake? A mental issue? The answers to these questions clear the way to instrument a proper exercise.

The exercises might addresses transition, footwork, speed, and placement issues. Yet, since the ultimate goal of the training is focused on maximizing the use of the best shot, the combination should be put together in such a fashion that would allow the player to manipulate an opponent so that it will be hard for the opponent to return the ball anywhere *except* the desired spot where the player can execute his best shot. Notice that the combination play does not seek out to win the point by any other shot earlier in the sequence, but merely producing an environment where the player is able to convert the point with his strongest shot.

Only a few training routines apart from learning mere strokes lies foundation of a high level player's development. The player's game is built on top of technical foundation, but it is reinforced with proper application. In time, new intangible skills emerge. A player's tactical and strategic thinking develop as a seamless byproduct of regular training. The only missing link is the ability look beyond the strokes.

I recall having a conversation with a player at my club regarding strokes. He was very frustrated and angry with himself after a loss to another player that he really wanted to beat. He wanted to practice with me so he could return my loops.

- "I just want to practice against your spin because when I played that guy, that's all he did and I could not block that ball. I simply don't have the stroke against that type of a spin ball."

- "Sure" I said, "But what kind of a shot did he do *before* that one?"

- "Well, he just pushed to the other side of the table, and then when I returned it, he spun the ball to the other side and while I reached the ball, I couldn't block it. He scored the point over and over."

- "We can train what you are asking me, but there is nothing wrong with your stroke and this type of training will not help you beat that guy", I said.

- "Why?" he asked me.

- "Because your opponent won that point earlier with the push."

In the words of Brad Gilbert, a professional tennis player who is best known for his exceptional skill understanding the game and winning without having the best of strokes on the pro circuit - "at some point, it is important to quit correcting the stroke and try to score some points."

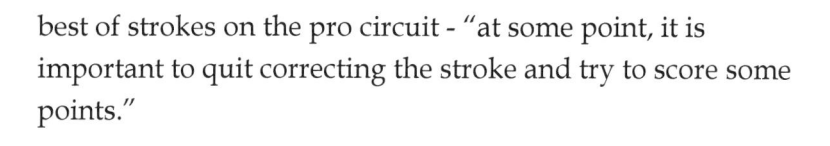

Reading the Game

I remember being upset after a loss because I was unable to reach the ball that my opponent looped wide to my forehand. No matter how early I seemed to make the leap to the ball, and how hard I tried, I was unable to touch the ball. I simply could not figure out why my opponent always reached a wide ball, while I did not. Was my adversary simply a faster athlete with much better reaction time or was I just significantly slower? The answers to my question were discovered quite quickly. Yet, it took quite a bit of time to learn to apply the knowledge needed to be able to reach that ball.

There are many books that describe the foundation of human reaction in sport. Matthew Syed, an English number one for many years, describes a service return challenge against tennis pro Michel Stitch in his book "Bounce." With his skills as table tennis player and his excellent career you would imagine that Matthew would be able to return or at least make contact with a tennis ball launched by the tennis pro. A large tennis court provides more time for reaction to incoming ball than the shots he has successfully returned standing nine feet away from his opponent in table tennis. However, the tennis pro continued to score an ace after an ace. If reaction is to blame and Matthew Syed was in fact a slower player, what would happen if we were to place the tennis pro on a table tennis court and offer him the same challenge? It is evident that the tables will turn and the tennis pro will seem to be a slower player. This means that one's reaction can only be measured against a known, specific action, instead of unfamiliar task. Place Matthew on the court for a few hours to continue watching opponent's serves against the tennis pro and soon Matthew would certainly be capable to return a few shots.

The reaction time is not a single measure of success and it is rarely the human element that is to blame for poor responses on the court. The measure of success, as noted by Mathew Syed in his book, "is the ability of the player not to see, but to perceive". The secret to success lies in the ability to read opponent's movements, recognizing the intention and responding with preemptive movement yourself. This preemptive movement ranges from changing position to cover certain placement areas or to recognize the type of spin or pace that will be produced by the stroke in order to adjust for the incoming ball. This is called anticipation.

There are many hints that can be used to read the opponent. First is the body movement. In table tennis, there are many elements of technique that must be sequentially executed in order to return a proper shot. If you understand the foundation of various techniques, you begin to recognize what spot the opponent chooses to aim his optimal shot, where he positions his feet, how he turns out his shoulders, and how far he goes for his backswing. All of these actions occur *before* the opponent even makes contact with the ball. These are the very actions that can be read and provide you with the information on the next shot to come.

The hardest part of the game is to learn how to recognize opponent's intent from his movements in order to *properly* anticipate the next move. Every opponent is different and some players are easier to read than others. Developing this skill takes experience and experience takes time. It is difficult to observe the opponent with peripheral vision since the focus is constantly on the ball. And while one can certainly develop this skill, there is an easier way to read the game.

Certainly, there are cunning techniques that exist to deceive the opponent by altering certain elements of technique during the approach to the shot. Yet, players are only human and that means that we can rely on our knowledge of human behavior and our knowledge of our training to approach this problem.

In table tennis, we achieve consistency of our skills through repetition. Once we achieve this consistency, we tend to perform the shot execution subconsciously. This means that the shot becomes a "grooved" action for a ball placed in a specific zone. Therefore, if a player is "offered" this type of a shot in a match, the response will most likely favor the placement and direction that has been thoroughly practiced. Altering the comfortable placement and direction requires activation of a conscious mind, which is a lot harder and error prone. In this environment, it is important to recognize the playing patterns the opponent prefers to execute and start playing on percentages.

In soccer, for example, every professional coach knows how important it is to keep track of opposite side's player statistics. Consider a striker getting ready for a penalty shot. Knowing how hard it is to score a single goal in soccer, the coach would certainly provide valuable feedback to the goalie regarding the striker's percentages.

Will he go right or left? In soccer, the distance between the striker and the goalie on the penalty shot is too short and the distance between posts is too large to be able to cover both directions at the same time. There is only a brief moment to determine whether to leap right or left. Frequently, the goalie simply takes an educated guess even before the striker gets ready to kick the ball. The educated guess is based on the knowledge of the striker's preferred shot. Surprisingly, even this simple statistic is responsible for quite a few victories.

The notion of player's statistics is soundly supported by science. If you look into the science behind a human being, you will find that our psychological predispositions are to attain comfort. We strive to achieve a balance in our comfort zones. These comfort zones are the elements that relax us. This is visible in many elements of our life - school, work, relationships. Frank Howard Clark, a screenwriter of the earlier 20th century, said that "a habit is something you can do without thinking - which is why most of us have so many of them." Human's behavior favors habits. Therefore, all players have certain habits in their movements and stroke executions[1]. Habits are created through repetition of tasks when our minds begin to respond to familiar tasks "automatically" using our subconscious mind.

Transposing this knowledge of human behavior to table tennis, we begin to realize that players have similar

---

[1] I prefer to call habits tendencies because the strongest of opponents do aim to vary their patterns on purpose in order to "mix up" their actions from their norm and due to intense training can do so effortlessly and consistently. However, they will still favor certain placements over others.

habits or tendencies when it comes to their strokes and placement choices. If you were to continuously place the ball in a certain spot for a given opponent, you will notice that the opponent has several "preprogrammed" responses. Statistically, the opponent's shot selection will favor one type of shot and the ball's placement over many other, even "preprogrammed" responses. These are the basics of percentage driven table tennis.

Instead of reading the opponent, a player can observe the opponent's responses and make a positive prediction on the opponent's shot selection, hence replacing anticipation with an educated guess. After all, you don't have to always be correct in your prediction of the opponent's shot, but as long as you are correct more times than you are mistaken, and you prepare to withstand the opponent's shot, you will begin to slowly gain the upper hand in the match. The only missing factor is your ability to cope with the opponent's shot without unforced errors.

The ability of properly predicting opponent's shot has other interesting advantages. Since both players read each other's movements, an opponent will also notice when you begin to move to cover their shot. Because preemptive movement starts before the ball even makes contact with opponent's paddle, the opponent might change his mind and decide to alter his placement at the last instant. But, how consistent is the opponent altering the placement when he attempts to execute a change of direction at the last moment? If the opponent's consistency is the same in many placement areas, you might just be out of luck, but for the most players, this will be an unlikely scenario. Even if a player struggles to return an opponent's shot, sometimes moving in to cover the angles of the incoming ball will bluff the opponent into attempting to send the ball to a different spot. The opponent will be required to engage his conscious mind to aim for a different placement. A few easy mistakes at this point of shot execution could be sufficient to turn the tide of the match.

The ability to read an opponent takes a lot of experience. Same goes for noting and recognizing opponent's tendencies. Often, a whole match will go by before the player finally understands opponent's playing patterns. Yet, it is a crucial skill in the roadmap for player's improvement to higher levels. At the beginner and intermediate levels, where players are not yet consistent enough even with their best shot, it may not even be necessary. For such players, immediate improvement will be gained once unforced errors are reduced. Yet, to improve further, this skill becomes very important.

Consider an opponent with a single killer shot to one spot that you're unable to reach, similarly to the initial dilemma I was facing in the match. If you continue struggling with a certain shot as I was, you will continuously see the same shot. Take a step into the opponent's shoes - why change a winning combination? The opponent can also play percentage table tennis by continually bombarding any specific spot as long as he scores more points than he loses. This is the double edged sword. Both players will try to read each other's actions and preferences. The winner of the match will be the player who is able to cope with opponent's shot with better consistency by being more prepared for an incoming shot and better capable to adjust to its variation. What will prompt the opponent to seek out alternative ways to gain the advantage is a player's ability to work with the opponent's shot without unforced errors.

While important, reading the game is not enough. It needs to be supported with proper technique. If a player is capable of reading the game and deciphering opponent's intentions, but is incapable of returning his shots due to poor technique, the technique will hamper the player's ability to come up with alternative responses to those shots.

In the beginner and intermediate levels, the players can begin to develop the skill of reading the game by observing and explaining what has just occurred on the court by asking themselves how the prior points ended and why. The best way to start doing so is during the practice matches with your training partners, coaches, and friends, the players that are willing to work with you on your improvement by helping you analyze your movements and shot selection whenever a mistake is made. Another alternative is capturing a video of your matches and training routines alike and evaluating your movements to identify areas most critical for improvement.

Dig deep into the details of the point, looking earlier than the final shot or the unforced error by analyzing the exchange of shots that led up to the end of the point. This type of analysis provides the deepest insight into the player's skills, both the strengths and the weaknesses. To advance further, the player has to know his own game and understand how to construct the points in the most favorable way for him or herself to score the point.

Action, Reaction

When I was a senior in high school, my friends used to hang out at a pool hall. This place was open all night long, a perfect spot where we could meet up after the movies, dinner, or a party. We liked to talk about everything happening in our lives over a game of billiards. We played for fun, but we did observe a couple pool sharks challenging each other a few times. What became immediately clear was that they almost never missed their shots! They were exceptionally good at putting practically any ball into a pocket and very skillful in properly assessing the position in order to send all other balls in a pocket without an error too.

Yet, there was more to their game. All of them had enough skill to hit a difficult shot. They were capable of hitting a difficult ball with the most fascinating spins and jumps, but what impressed us the most was the gracefulness of how they could line up almost every ball in a sequence for simple and very obvious subsequent shot. A shot so simple, they would never miss. These pool sharks were not just concerned with the action of placing the ball into the pocket, but also how the cue ball would react *after* the shot so that it would deflect and roll into a spot most suitable for the next shot. Consequently, the better player was not the one with the best shot, but the one with better ability to properly select a next ball to send into a pocket. That was a secret to their game!

Does the same principle apply in table tennis?

Absolutely! In table tennis, we do not control all the shots so that they line up like the ducks in a row for a much easier win, but we surely can influence the opponent to give us an easier shot every now and then. Smart player that pays attention to what is happening on the court will begin to recognize that there are certain shots that will force the opponent to produce an expected response. A shot so easy, that any player can take advantage of the opportunity in order to win the next point.

    The key to continuously producing these types of opportunities is by realizing the opponent's patterns and choosing the type of placement that is awkward for the opponent. From an awkward position, for example, the opponent is forced to try to simply keep the point alive, either popping up an easy ball every once in a while or producing the ball with a much reduced and predictable spin. This is one of the obvious examples.

    Indeed, there are common patterns in table tennis that occur more often than others simply due to the fact that most players train in a very similar manner and they produce the same responses for the same situation. Since forehand training remains the primary element in table tennis for every beginner and intermediate player, the sequences of shots around long pushes deep to the body of the opponent and deep and wide to the forehand, when done randomly, usually produce unforced errors or easy balls that can be put away on the next shot. These types of long pushes can be best applied during service returns and are the key tactics that better players use against lower level players. On the backhand, deep sidespin pushes that move the ball wider away from the backhand tend to produce the same problems for the players since the ball, ideally received by the opponent off the bounce, curves slightly wider. If the opponent does not properly assess the ball's side spin trajectory, he may attempt either to fish, or push the ball back on the table with a bit margin for error, making the ball easier to attack.

A wide backhand zone is also a good area to exploit with spin. Most players do not move wide to the backhand with the same ease as they move to the forehand. Player's reach on the backhand side is a lot shorter and in order for players to hit an offensive backhand correctly, the player should move to be in front of the ball. Therefore a ball placed wide to the backhand area often produces a passive response from the opponent. Such passive response provides an opportunity to score the point with a strong consecutive shot.

The principle of action, reaction can be also applied by looking at the opponent's tendencies. If the opponent consistently blocks a loop instead of countering it, and especially if the opponent is very careful with the block and does not vary its placement, you can take advantage of this reaction by slowing down your loop in order to win the point by driving the blocked ball on the next shot instead of blindly trying to go through the player's block early in the opening shot.

What about footwork patterns? Some players make a mistake of assuming that the ball is farther from them than it truly is. Instead of waiting and smoothly moving in to the optimal position, players rush to get to a wide ball with a cross step that moves a player a lot farther than an ideal stroke requires. While cross step is a good footwork technique to develop allowing the player to move farther for a very wide ball, yet this technique carries way too much body weight sideways. The momentum generated through this type of movement requires a significant shift in balance making it difficult to recover to the ready position. If the step is taken too close to the table, the player does not have enough time to recover the balance and will be unable to use a forehand on a next shot to the body. Frequent symptom of this position is a less offensive or a desperate backhand shot from a far forehand corner. This shot comes out because the player overran his ideal position. A player that finds himself in this position is usually struggles to recover quickly to the ready position and frequently gets locked to the forehand size of the table unable to change direction to cover even the easiest shot to the backhand. Players with this type of a technical flaw in footwork and positioning can be forced to produce this type of a reaction with a simple, soft wide ball.

  Playing against certain type of blockers is yet another way to anticipate the reaction and take advantage of your opponent's patterns. Blockers are one of the most difficult types of players to beat because they can really make some players look darn silly by continually placing the ball in various corners of the table. Blockers deserve a lot of respect for their skill. Yet, some blockers really fall in love with this type of tactic; they keep returning the ball right and left, right and left. Usually this pattern is driven by one very basic concept in the game – place the ball into an open area, making the opponent move. If you constantly try to get to the ball and just bring it back trying to rush yourself early to get to the other corner, you will be playing the blocker's game, reacting in a way favorable to your opponent. But if you leave the emotions and the pressures out of the point and recognize that the blocker is creating wide angles because blockers generally do not want to move, you can take advantage of these angles using slow spin in order to produce an even sharper angle for your opponent, forcing the blocker out of his element and having him or her reach for a wide, slow ball and giving up their solid position and quick blocks from the middle of the table.

Choppers are probably the best players who understand the concept of action and reaction. They constantly feed a specific type of a ball to the attacker and based on the shot they produce, they are able to determine what their approach to the next ball should be. Modern defenders, who are able to attack as well as defend, rely on their ability to read the next ball in order to go on an offensive. If a chopper produces a very low ball that is relatively short and carries very little spin, the attacker will most likely have to push the ball back. Those pushes are very difficult to push back low and short and frequently pop up higher and trail deeper than desired. Once the chopper observes that he produced low chop, he begins to anticipate the attacker's weaker push by moving closer to the table in order to get ready to take advantage of the opportunity to attack.

Another example of choppers using their superior understanding of reaction comes out of my own experience. Two of my strongest adversaries for a very long time were choppers. My loop of an underspin ball was improving, allowing me to sustain the pressure on my opponents. I aimed to loop the ball wider and wider to the backhand, forcing my opponents to move away from the table. My strategy over time grooved the timing of my stroke to produce a consistent attack to the backhand. With that, I felt awkward dynamically changing the direction of my loop to attack the forehand. I became very predictable. Both choppers began to notice my reaction after an initial attack to their backhand and even the after next shot in the sequence. I was locked in a pivot position around my backhand corner, ready to make another pivot with a wider angle. The choppers exploited the opportunity I presented with my position by chopping the ball into the forehand zone right at the moment when I began to pivot wider.

    I was consistently caught unprepared. Off balance, forced to change direction of my movement in a very quick instance, I frequently lost the point in an error. I was constantly surprised seeing the opponents continue to put the ball to my strongest side. To me, it seemed unlikely that someone would just place the ball right into my forehand. What I did not realize is that my movement was so overly obvious that it created an opportunity for my opponents instead. Once I began to watch my opponent's action *before* moving and especially after improving my footwork and timing for my cross court loop against an underspin ball, my opponents were no longer able to force me to make an easy mistake.

    Let's look at the action, reaction principle applied to a service return. Your opponent delivers a serve with a spin that you are not able to clearly read and the ball pops up high after a push allowing your opponent to win the point. You continually see the opponent delivering the same serve as you struggle with the response. Wouldn't you try to make an adjustment? How would you make the adjustment? Are you going keep stabbing at the ball with the push, trying to keep the ball lower, or will you recognize that the ball is popping up and therefore, it is probably not underspin and that you should try roll the ball back instead? Will you adapt by changing your reaction or will you produce a slightly improved or rather improvised push return where your opponent already demonstrated his ability to put away shot after shot?

I think these questions are rhetorical, but I am certain some of the readers begin to recognize themselves as the stubborn players unable to make an adjustment to their reaction when the play demands it.

The fact of the matter is that if you are aware of your strengths and weaknesses, with a little emphasis and the analysis of the point, you can begin to recognize the patterns that play out throughout the match. The patterns will be reoccurring. Opponent's predictable reactions can be favorably exploited. Likewise, your own reactions can be tweaked to be less predictable in order to gain an upper hand and win.

Kareem Abdul-Jabbar once said "You can't win unless you learn how to lose." If you learn *how* you lose the points, you can certainly figure out how to win at least some of them.

The Best Technique

A lot of players get very caught up with the question of what kind of technique is superior. Obviously the desire for the players to get to the bottom of the question is their aim to learn the "right" technique that will lead them to the green pastures where these players will shine with their amazing technical skills by beating every player that stands in the way. The quest to learn the best technique sounds logical. Unfortunately, it is a myth.

Certainly some readers will object, "But wait a minute, how about Chinese team being the strongest in the world, their technique must be the best. Look at their dominance!" True. Chinese domination is very impressive. China is able to produce world class table tennis athletes in such great numbers and with such great strengths, that it would be reasonable to assume that their technique is superior. Yet, there are other facts that play a vital reason in Chinese National Team domination. Chinese table tennis achievements cannot be blindly credited only due to technique.

Let's take a look at any European player whose technique generally looks a lot different from his Chinese adversaries and assume that there is a special Chinese technique that is only taught to Chinese National Team players. Wouldn't a Chinese coach be able to teach the European player the "better" technique? Certainly. Human brains and human body in our day and age are known to have the same abilities regardless of player's country of origin, race, or ethnic background. In this case, it would be possible for the European player to play with a Chinese taught technique and dominate the world arena, but then why are there so few European players that seem to visually display the same technical execution as the Chinese players? Coaches and players from China have been immigrating to other parts of the world in search of a better life and careers. These individuals participated and coached in various leagues, clubs, and associations around the world. They would surely have made their mark visible by producing players possessing the same visible strokes as the one they have been exposed to during their career. We do not quite see this type of impact from the technical standpoint. Why?

    The answers again lie within the foundation of the rigorous training of the Chinese players in comparison with the European counterparts. China's training program is very strong and the players are put under the enormous training, repeating shot after shot to perfection. Spin, speed, footwork, service return - all elements are worked on with high level of pressure on the players to continuously produce results or be replaced by the next player in line with a harder work ethic and a stronger mental game. In the end, the players that surface are the cream of the crop, the best players in the world, who possess many strengths grooved through the unforgiving training. One of such strengths is timing and how to apply timing in the match in order to win.

    Timing is one of the most important elements of

technique. In order to have the type of timing possessed by the Chinese players, the footwork and stroke execution must be perfected to a level that to amateur players seems almost inhuman. Thus, the reason why European players do not resemble the same visual characteristic of technique is that their training from the early stages has not been focused on the same elements as the Chinese training to satisfy the timing demands of the Chinese grown technique.

Historically, European players do not have such aggressive training converting the youth into world class players. Originally, European players train in isolation, under a supervision of one coach who develops the player's early game. If the success is visible for this player, the player is moved to a different club, league or organization continuing his training under the supervision of another coach, then by another coach, until he reaches a high level. This type of player development "program" is much uncoordinated through the player's development and forces the next level coaches to work with the strokes that the player adopts early in his career and tweak the technique to make it better instead of completely dismantling it and teaching a different technique from the start[2].

---

[2] You might notice that I use the word "strokes" and "technique" interchangeably. Both words have the same meaning in the context of this chapter. Yet, there are clearly differences. Strokes or shots are merely the visual representation of the motions, while technique is more subtle. It involves visible and hidden elements during the shot. For example, the wrist can be delicately applied during the stroke altering ball's behavior upon contact. Therefore, strokes are derived from technique by applying a certain type of action on the ball, which in turn is produced by a specific movement. These movements are the core of the player's ability to play shots with vastly different spins and numerous placements and they are rigorously practiced in training.

Contrasting the quality of the European player development with Chinese table tennis youth development program, the differences are vast. Top Chinese kids from towns get transitioned to city sport schools which follow established table tennis curriculum. The kids at the top of their class then get promoted to Provincial B teams, then Provincial A teams. Eventually, the top candidates from 31 Provinces in China make up the National B team, from where 24 will eventually make up the National A team. That is a humongous and continuous pool of top quality players.

Training differences aside, both European and Chinese players are capable of reaching the top 20 players in the world despite their differences in technique. Obviously the Chinese training program is much stronger due to its large influx of kids that come in and high number of great players that come out of the program, while the lack of smooth transition for the European player in various stages of the development produces a much fewer number of individuals able to compete at the world class arena. Despite this, the technique is unlikely to be blamed for the lack of European success on the world stage. The reason for this is that technique is what teaches the players the knowledge behind the stroke execution, but it is not what wins the game!

Close your eyes and think about your toughest matches. Do you remember a match where your opponent was giving you a type of a shot you simply could not handle? Maybe it was an attack you could not block even though you were ready for the ball, or a counter you kept missing, or even an easy popped up ball. This is where the holes in the technique become visible - when there are shots that the opponent produces create all kinds of problems for the player. A typical example of such technical holes is an attacking player not being able to cope with the shots produced by a long pip blocker. This type of an opponent forces the attacking player to approach the ball with more touch, stretching the footwork demands and patience to the maximum.

In words of Bruno Walter "by concentrating on precision, one arrives at technique, but by concentrating on technique, one doesn't arrive at precision." This means that the technique is what allows the player to make a desired shot. Technique is what delivers the type of a shot with a desired pace, spin, and placement. However, blindly working on technique does not guarantee that there will be a purpose for it. For example, during my competitions I frequently have seen my lower level opponents attempting to use backhand flips against serves that were much too strong for their skill level. Serve after serve, I was awarded easy points. The opponents stubbornly attempted to "practice" their technique, which was obviously too weak for the level they were competing. If one is practicing, one must aim to perfect the technique, but if one is competing, one must aim to win!

If there is no best technique, why even work on it? And if you work on it, what should you learn? Technique provides a strong foundation for the player to continue improving. Every element depends on technique, but the strength lies in technique's flexibility. It does not matter whether it influences your stokes to bear a resemblance to a specific professional international player of a certain origin, but what matters is that you should be able to apply the technique to approach even the most difficult of shots in the game with success. The comparison of poor technique would be a musician that does not have a good technique for playing an instrument while attempting to write the musical piece played with that instrument. He might be able to write the notes, but it will be very difficult and awkward to play them. So difficult, that mastering the musical piece would be practically impossible.

Possessing a good technique opens up a lot of opportunities to the player. Let's look at some examples from tennis, table tennis' "bigger" brother. Alexandr Dolgopolov, top-ranked Ukrainian tennis player once said "I had a classic technique - one of the best techniques when I was like 10, 12, but then I changed." Alexandr is considered an unorthodox all-around tennis player who is pronounced as the most deceptive players on the tennis pro tour, frequently driving his opponents crazy with his unpredictable placement, drop shots, and variations. What allowed him to become such a difficult opponent was the technical background he has learned at an early age. With his background, he was able to figure out how to vary his shot execution and approach to a shot without telegraphing his intentions to the opponent. Alexandr's game was built around his technical strengths by using it as the flexible framework that was purposefully modified to allow him to play the game significantly different than any other player on the pro tour. What about table tennis?

In our sport, every player in the top 20 has

something very unique about his game. Certainly the world class players possess all the shots, but they have certain specialty shots that make them stand out and cause problems to many other players in the lower ranks aiming to break into the top spots. For some players, it's their backhands, defense, off the bounce countering, wild placements, strong spin combinations, service, consistency, speed, power, etc. All these elements are different for every player. As a matter of fact, if you were to teach an element of technique to several players at once, each and every one of these players would execute it differently, but each player's concepts behind the stroke execution would be identical.

Allen Fox in his book "Think to win" states the following - "… is proper stroke technique simply a matter of individual preference or are some techniques better for everyone in all cases? I would answer that there are, in fact, easier as well as more difficult ways of hitting the ball… The differences in the way professional players hit the ball prove only that great athletes who work hard enough can do things the hard way and still be effective." I undoubtedly agree with this statement.

There is no substitute for good technique. There are also no shortcuts to learn the technique the easy way either. The reason table tennis has more beginner and intermediate players than advanced players is because of the very fact that it is very hard to learn and develop the technique for every player. The reason there are many different styles exist in table tennis is because some players find it much more difficult to learn a specific type of technique and choose to play the game using their current, present skills.

The good news is that technique can be learned and developed. It is best learned in stages, as a multi-tiered cake. Foundation forms the base. Then, all other tiers begin to reside one on top of the other, until eventually you put the cherry on top. To improve, the player does not need to be concerned with only learning the best technique because there is no such thing. The best technique is the one perfected by the player, adapted to suit the player's style, knowledge, understanding, and the strengths - a technique that can be effectively applied as a solution to the ever changing environment playing out on the court.

Control

A common term used in table tennis is control, yet it is surprising to find that many players in various levels do not understand this term or its importance in the sport. Most amateurs, for example, believe that control implies equipment. Yet, control is not just a number you read on the table tennis blade or rubber advertising. Control is a measure of the player's ability to cope with opponent's shots. It is defined by technique. Good control means that the player is able to find the means to return a given shot.

A player can certainly improve the control with practice, but how do you improve your control during the match when the result of the match really depends on it? The secret is to possess the knowledge of the stroke technique and understand which elements of technique influence your control of the shots.

When the player moves in to hit the ball, the player performs various movements. These movements are done in a sequence. For a right handed player, the player aiming to hit a forehand shot will first approach the ball, positioning himself within the comfortable distance so that the contact will be made within the striking zone - area within the player's comfortable reach. While the player is approaching the ball, he will execute a backswing. Then, the player will begin rotating his body to generate the transfer of weight. The weight transfer will begin from the legs, followed by the torso, hips, shoulders, eventually releasing the arm to strike the ball.

The transfer of weight is initiated by the feet. The balance shifts as the feet rotate on the balls of the foot. During the rotation, the hips and the rest of the body follow. Then, the body begins to pull the right shoulder, which in turn, makes the right arm begin to move forward. The forearm will accelerate very quickly a moment right before the contact with the ball is made. Ideally, the contact with the ball is made when the forearm reaches its maximum velocity, also called a forehand snap. During the contact of the ball, the wrist will naturally curl around the ball as the arm follows through to the finishing position. The final stage is the follow through of the arm as the body begins to slow down its motion while still carrying the body forward to the stroke's ending position. Then, the body decelerates the rotation followed by the relaxing of the arm and the recovery motion back into the neutral position guided again with the body movement similar to the one that initiated the stroke.

This is a thorough description of the body movements during execution of a forehand loop. The way the body produces the shot is what derives control. The key to improving control is by understanding the role of each movement in the sequence. Some movements directly impact control, while others are responsible for other tasks and have less of an impact on the overall control, but instead contribute to other variables of a table tennis shot like timing and power. If you are aware which movements allow you to raise the control of your shots and which movements reduce control instead, you can make adjustments to your stroke to help you manage your opponent's shots with better chances for success.

Before starting to look at the body's motion and identify which movements in the sequence have the biggest significance in the stroke, we need to review a very basic principle - what makes the ball move?

Certainly hitting the ball will make it fly forward. This is called impact. The nature of the physics behind table tennis is the same for every sport that is using a ball. It is based on the principles of acceleration, momentum, and energy. I will not dive into the physics formulas as it is not the purpose of this book, but the main concept that needs to be considered is that the ball does not care how the energy is transferred into it to make it move. Whether you apply a gentle touch or a violent blow, the ball will move forward. The only difference that will matter for control is how *accurately* someone can deliver an appropriate amount of energy in order to continuously move the ball a desired length of distance and how to apply a proper amount of spin to create a desired trajectory of the flight of the ball that would greatly increase the chances of placing the ball on the table.

The purpose of this chapter is to define elements of control and how to properly apply them in the game. Therefore we are only concerned with the ability to repeat the same type of shot over and over with consistent, predictable results.

Every beginner that took a piece of advice in table

tennis from a coach or a friend probably heard these words "move your feet." This is the most uttered phrase in table tennis training. It does not mean move just anywhere, it implies two crucial actions necessary for a stroke. First, is the approach to the ball and the second is the balance transfer during the stroke. Obviously the approach aspect of the foot movement is needed in order to be able to make contact with the ball. Without stepping to the ball, the player will either reach to the ball or lean away from it. Reaching for the ball and cramped strokes will obviously cause problems for the player in numerous aspects, consequently being a reason why the opponent's try to target the wide and close to the body areas. What about balance transfer?

Balance transfer is probably the most important element in table tennis. Balance transfer is achieved with movement of the feet. The feet rotate on the ball of each foot, accompanied with the rotation of the hips (obviously in a stance where the knees are bent, straight knees will impede all kinds of movement). This movement ensures stability. But what does the balance transfer or the feet have to do with control?

This is exactly the question that is frequently ignored. Clearly, the feet do not make contact with the ball, nor does the body during the balance transfer. Where does then the balance fit into the control formula?

Let's do an experiment. Stick your arm to your side with your paddle in the hand. Lock your wrist so that it does not move. Tuck the elbow to your side and lock it in place as well so that neither the arm nor the forearm moves during the stroke, but relax your body a bit so you are not too stiff.

Now, if you can have someone feed the ball to you so that you do not have to reach to the ball, but merely make contact with the ball as you transfer your balance, you will see that you will consistently produce the same shot as long as you are receiving the same type of ball and make contact with it at the same timing point. This shot will likely not only have the same feel, but will have the same length, spin, and placement. This shows that the balance transfer or the "movement of feet" is very important in achieving control, but there seems to be no direct relationship to control since there is no direct contact with the ball. As a matter of fact, balance transfer is much more vital in the production of power and in the recovery back to the ready position, which are directly dependent on the player's ability to transfer the weight and maintain the balance during the stroke execution. However, let's continue our experiment.

  Attempt to transfer the balance faster or slower as you make contact with the ball and you will see the length of your shot beginning to vary, but the ball will continue moving to the same direction. If the direction of the ball changes, it is likely that you have included the next element into the motion - the rotation of the shoulders, which is the next element that has a relationship on control. (In the previous exercise, we did not purposefully try to eliminate the movement of the shoulders from the stroke because the motion of balance transfer naturally involves the rotation of the torso.) The shoulders do not really rotate, they are static, but what rotates is the body at the waist. The rotation of the waist changes the way the shoulders are positioned when a person is facing a certain direction and that is the element that we will analyze next in our experiment.

The shoulders have the arm attached directly to it, but in our experiment, the arm is fixed with an elbow locked at the side. When the body rotates, the arm swings. If the rotation is longer and carries the shoulder of the hitting arm farther, the ball will go wider. If the rotation halts earlier than desired, the contact with the ball will be made earlier and the ball will go straighter. For the sake of our experiment, let's try to hit the ball by rotating the torso (and hence the shoulders) with the arm, elbow and wrist remaining locked, but without using the feet. What you will find is that it is very difficult to accelerate and decelerate the rotation. Without the extra acceleration, the pace of the ball will be greatly reduced in comparison with the weight transfer motion. The shoulders turn relatively fast for only a small range of motion, but larger ranges of motion necessary for extra power is hard to achieve in fixed stance. The rotation of the body at the waist is therefore good for directional movement of the ball, but it does not deliver the necessary power for a strong shot. As a matter of fact, if you get a slow ball, you will be very unlikely to hit it with enough pace to clear the net, however if you receive a fast incoming shot, you would be capable of deflecting it easily using only the waist rotation. With this exercise it is easy to conclude that the waist rotation seems to be responsible for the direction of the ball travel and is also a good element to control body's movement during a block of a fast shot, where the body acts as a soft frame to deflect a fast shot and absorb incoming power and pace due to its limited range of motion.

Now, we will look at the forearm. I am certain that you have heard the term "whip action." The "whip action" described talks about the body's ability to contract muscles to accelerate the movement, therefore allowing creation of a large amount of force in a sequential interaction of various body parts and engagement of their respective muscle groups. This is also referred to as the biomechanical elasticity.[3] If we revisit the rotation of the torso without using the legs and allow you to extend your arm back slightly by loosening up the elbow so that the elbow is no longer fixed from movement, you will notice that the torso will rotate with a much more explosive action. As the arm is brought further back, it creates a large amount of energy through the elasticity of the muscles which produce a great deal of force as the muscles begin to contract during the stroke. This type of arm's motion is called a backswing which is clearly responsible for generating the power in a stroke.

Yet, the forearm is responsible for another element of the stroke. Straighten your arm and do not allow the arm to bend at the elbow while executing the stroke you will notice how awkward the stroke will begin to look. Not only does this movement with a straight arm slows down the stroke eliminating the "whip action", this type of a stroke is also

---

[3] Biomechanical elasticity describes human muscle groups and the way they work together. Our muscles do not have any abilities to push. They are only designed to pull. That is why our bodies have two sets of muscle groups pulling in two opposite directions. In order for movement to occur, one of the muscles has to relax to stretch and the other has to contract. Because of this fact, to achieve a high speed intensity movement, we require prior relaxation and retraction of one muscle and a speedy contraction of the other. A typical example of this is visible in shots that are executed with the backswing – backswing has to occur before the contact is made. The trick however, is to execute the backswing at a right time before the forward swing is executed. Otherwise, if the player awaits in backswing position for too long, the body will lose the elastic energy created by the backswing and it will be harder to execute a forward swing.

extremely long, producing many problems for recovery into a ready position. The gracefulness of the motion no longer exists and the balance of the body is completely disrupted. The forearm is responsible for "braking" after the shot execution, decelerating the stroke with the very bending of the elbow on the follow through.

Now we have reached the wrist, which is the most flexible part of the body during the stroke execution. Can you hit the ball with the wrist only without using any other parts of the body? Of course, but the consistency of a wrist only shot will likely be poor. The wrist is extremely agile and its control is difficult to achieve. This is why the touch game so vital for service return remains one of the hardest elements of the game to master. However, because the wrist is so quick and flexible, it can be bent in a way to return a ball containing very wide variation of spins. In addition, the flexibility of the wrist allows the player to apply different types of brushing motions during the contact with the ball that in turn can generate different types of spin. Thus, the wrist is responsible for generating spin on touch shots on top of being responsible for rotating to cover the angles necessary to return the incoming shots. The wrist, however, is also capable of applying additional power to the stroke as well when it is directly guided to strike the back of the ball, rather than executing a somewhat brushing motion around the ball.

Finally, we have the hand and fingers. The hand and fingers are used to hold the paddle. We will not analyze different types of grips and how the grips influence control, but there is one element worth considering that is important for all grips: how tight is the grip. Tight grip produces a much stronger rebound of the ball on impact, while loose grip catches the ball with finer touch and absorbs incoming power of the ball. Changing the tightness of the grip allows the player to fine tune the response according with the demands of the play when it could be too late to alter other elements of the stroke.

Recapping on the details of the abovementioned paragraphs, we begin to draw a better understanding of the elements of control. Power and balance are controlled by the feet, waist rotation, and the forearm. The shoulders and the arm (with the angle of the elbow bend) are responsible for the general direction of the ball's movement after impact. Wrist and the hands are responsible for the micro motions of the stroke which impart the spin and manage angles needed to return shots of various types of spin and speed.

How does one apply this knowledge in the game? During the game, even the easiest of shots can be missed. Does one brush it off and say to himself that mistakes are nothing but a fluke? Certainly, unforced errors are common, but if several shots are missed in the row, especially as a response to opponent's continuous deliver of a specific shot, it is likely that the player needs to diagnose what he can do in order to improve the quality of his response. This is where knowledge of control comes in.

Here are a few examples. A player returns a slow topspin service and misses the table. The player can try to approach the same serve again with the same action not knowing what exactly went wrong during the stroke or he could eliminate the use of the wrist by locking the wrist and brushing up on the ball with a slower motion using only the forearm. He may still miss, but after eliminating the elements of the stroke that are most flexible, he improves control, which is what is needed in order to increase the likelihood of returning the shot.

If the loop drive of a spiny shot goes long, should one swing harder and disregard the mistake hoping to get lucky on the next attempt or should the player reduce the backswing of the loop drive and lock the wrist to improve the control when the same type of ball again occurs during the match?

If the player blocks the ball off the table, should he do the same thing and hope to make a consecutive shot or should he consider relaxing the hands and soften up the grip absorbing the incoming pace of the ball (obviously assuming the blocking angle is properly set)?

In all of the described scenarios, the player can choose to ignore the errors and continue playing without an adjustment. Yet, it might be too late and too difficult to come up with the proper response under pressure of a game or a match. It's best to gain a proper understanding of all the elements that control the stroke and be capable of making changes when the time comes – changes that might not completely eliminate all the difficulties of the match and grant you a win but at the very least give you the tools to put up a tougher resistance.

Let's revisit the prior chapter on the best technique and apply the principles of control to fine tune a definition of a superior technique. We will find that the best technique is usually the type of technique that is sufficiently agile to raise a level of control on a desired shot. Matthew Syed provides a great insight into his training focused on improving technique in his book "Bounce", where he was lucky enough to work with Chen Xinhua to enrich the technical strengths of his game. Chen Xinhua made a major adjustment in Mathew's technique not to make it stronger or more consistent, but in order for his technique to be reproducible, providing "the perfect conditions for feedback." In words of Chen offered by Matthew in his book, "If you don't know what you are doing wrong, you can never know what you are doing right." The emphasis of the phrase is that the technique needs to be strong enough to produce the same quality shot with wide application, but agile enough that it can be controlled through the feedback in order to make necessary adjustments.

    A technique that limits the player from making necessary adjustments impedes player's ability to fine tune control. With lack of control, player's responses begin to fork over the initiative and the match outcome to the opponent. "I might win, or I might not" mentality by blindly going for shots without any regard for errors is a poor long term strategy. Knowing how to correct one's actions, the results will no longer be decided by sheer luck. My coach, Gerald Reid, always says "Luck favors the prepared." Understanding the elements of the stroke and having a methodical approach towards problem solving is exactly what it means to be prepared.

Power and Control

Mastering the strokes comes with a realization that the best of the attacking shots strongly depend on the amount of power supplied into the stroke. Therefore, the intention, if the opportunity presents itself, is to apply the maximum power into a stroke with maximum control of the placement. Yet, power and control are two absolutely opposing principles, as maximizing either of them means diminishing the quality of another.

To deliver maximum power, the paddle needs to reach a maximum velocity during its contact with the ball. To supply the maximum velocity into a stroke, the body is put under a heavy stress, demanding all the body parts to move in unison to produce the energy required to propel the ball forward. However, the large number of moving body parts involved in the stroke mechanism cause the body to lose its fine tuned interaction. Timing gets out of synch. With maximum power, the movements become longer. The longer movements compromise balance and usually lead to inadequate deceleration necessary for stroke recovery. The feeling of the ball during contact does not provide the adequate feedback during powerful strokes either as the body is rushed to generate more power sooner. Shots requiring maximum power are high risk. With significant complications in stoke recovery and balance, these shots are best applied as winners.

When trying to optimize control, the opposite occurs.

You attempt to eliminate extra elements of the stroke to maintain control, which takes away additional energy necessary for larger power feed. As a matter of fact maximum control is achieved when the paddle is completely static. This can be demonstrated if you use a table tennis robot that produces the same shot with identical speed, spin and placement. These identical shots can be returned back by statically holding the paddle in a spot where the angle suits the incoming ball's spin as long as desired. The instance one attempts to alter the type of the return shot or the placement of the return shot by striking the incoming ball, the timing aspects begin to take affect and the chances of an error begin to increase.

Hence, power and control are completely opposed.[4] Both cannot be maximized as one yields to diminished capacity of the other, which means that the player must carefully apply either one or the other depending on the opportunities that come up during the rally. The solution, therefore, is to find a happy medium where the shots are delivered with largest amount of power that allows maintaining the highest level of control[5].

Table tennis, however, is a sport of ever-changing

---

[4] Interesting to note that greater control is achieved with maximum spin as it produced a much improved arch for the trajectory of the ball. Greater spin in turn is produced with greater input of power.

[5] One of the best ways to maximize both power and control while still engaging all of the body movement is done by smooth acceleration of a relaxed body. The shot produced with relaxed body increases the control while complete use of the body produces a lot more power. Incidentally, this type of an approach to a stroke also improves timing as the body is not rushed to produce a shot quickly.

environment. The ball produced by the opponent will always vary in many aspects. How can someone continuously deliver the shots within the range of highest power input with highest level of control at the same time? This is best explained by Allen Fox in his book "Think to win." While the book is written on tennis, the principles behind tennis ground strokes identify the same aspects of technique as the strokes in table tennis.

Allen Fox writes that there are four sources of power, all of which need to be engaged in order to produce the shot with maximum power. The first source of power is legs, second, shoulder and upper body, third comes from moving the arm relative to the shoulder, and finally the wrist.

If we were to compare these sources of power with areas of control defined in the experiment section of the prior chapter, it becomes clear that each element of the stroke that was "turned off" in the examples of player's adjustments in order to maximize control are the same elements that are responsible for delivering extra power into the stroke. How can this knowledge be applied?

Look at some of the professional matches among the top table tennis players in the world. You will see how they seem to maintain the balance of power during their exchanges. Even when they are out of position, they are capable of placing the ball accurately and offensively back on the table. Matches show how the professionals seem to use the wrist in order to supply the power to a stroke in an awkward, almost desperate situation to recover the rally back in their favor. The matches also show how the fastest recovery times come from shorter strokes, which is exactly what allows the players to maintain a high degree of consistency, but those strokes do not become less effective as they still deliver a strong punch by borrowing the power mostly for the legs and shoulders. On touch shots, requiring the extra finesse, such as forehand flicks and flips, the pros deliver unbelievable amount of power by lunging their body forward to serve as the extra body of mass to feed the ball with the energy required to thrust the ball forward, which without sufficient power would immediately fly into the net.

Thus, the power element is yet another piece of the puzzle that helps the player determine an appropriate response to a shot. This knowledge also helps establish a long term vision for further refinement and optimization of the stroke's efficiency, consistency, and effectiveness.

Spin and Speed

To appreciate table tennis, one has to love spin. Attackers are enamored with their loops, while defenders are thrilled to see floating, low underspin chops, or "dancing" through the air, unpredictable no spin shots. Same goes for speed. Some players want to win points based on speed of their shots, while others prefer to spin the ball. However, when looking at the way a player aims to score the points, these elements yet again counter balance each other similarly to power and control.

Speed is achieved through direct transfer of energy into the ball, while spin is created with a brush motion of the paddle against the ball. As more spin is being produced, less energy is supplied into the forward direction of the ball. However, unlike power and control aimed to achieve happy medium by applying maximum power with maximum control to all the shots, the speed and spin characteristics depends more on the type of the incoming ball and what kind of a shot you are trying to produce. If you are reaching for a late ball, for example, it would be best to try to put more spin on the ball and slow the shot down to give yourself time to get into a recovery position, rather than try to maximize the speed of the shot and go for a high risk winner.

This type of analysis derives a very basic question. What type of a shot should the player strive to make if presented with an obvious reasonable choice in shot selection? A shot with more spin, a shot with higher speed, or try the blend of the two?

This is a question that does not have a definite answer as it largely depends on the player's and the opponent's strengths and weaknesses. Yet, if we assume both players possess the necessary skills to apply a fast and spiny shot alike, we can determine a hierarchy of the importance by looking at the way the professionals play the game and looking into the future trends of the sport.

The larger ball introduced more than a decade ago forced the players to stand closer to the table in order to deliver the same amount of power on the shots. The speed of the ball will therefore have a lot more impact to the opponent's ability to find suitable responses for highs speed shots due to the time limitations that exist at short distance between players. The plans of the International Table Tennis Federation to introduce a plastic seamless ball into the sport supposedly will make it harder for players to create spin as well. Thus, with these two variables at play, it is probably best to tailor the game in an attempt to maximize the speed of the ball. Looking at the older traditions of the sport and attempting to build the game solely around spin means not keeping up with the time and may become an ineffective long term vision.

On the contrary, if we begin to build the game around speed, where does the spin come into the picture? The spin is still a very necessary element as it allows the players to attack a low ball by lifting it over the net in an arch so that the ball would clear the net and still hit the table.

However, there are some other very interesting observations that can be made in regards to speed and spin.

The strongest of the spins are created when the paddle is brushing against the ball with a maximum speed. As long as this motion keeps gripping the ball, the ball will be given a maximum amount of energy through the spin. Such spin has the ability to accelerate on impact with the table and hence introduces a much more difficult shot for the opponent to handle. The bounce of the ball is quite unpredictable due to the amount of actual spin on the ball and the angle of deflection at impact with the table set by the ball's trajectory. However, a faster shot with less spin is still very effective, especially if the ball is low. Blocking or countering this shot requires producing a slight lift to clear the ball over the net or opening the paddle angle, which is very hard to accurately accomplish in a time constrained situation. If the impact of high speed, flatter shot is not absorbed well by the receiver, the ball kicks and travels out of bounce, but if the angle on the blade is closed as if returning stronger topspin ball before contact, the ball will likely fly into the net.

Thus, speed and spin play a much more important role in the variety of the application of both elements within a rally. When the opponent is close to the table and under pressure you have a better chance to win the point by going for a faster shot, assuming recovery for the next shot is not compromised. On the same note if the opponent gives you a shot challenging your ability to quickly respond to it, such as a fast push wide or directly into the body, the shot with more spin is likely to be an appropriate solution.

When evaluating spin and speed of a shot, there are a few other dimensions that need to be considered in shot selection. Faster, flatter shots require the face of the racket to be open and hence have a larger surface to contact the ball, reducing a chance of a missed hit. Topspin strokes that start with a closed angle generally have a larger margin of error in that regard because the closed angle of the paddle necessary for topspin strokes minimizes the surface area of the racket.

The application of higher spin also requires more energy to be applied into the brush portion of the stroke, which in turn requires more strength. Allen Fox said it best - "[topspin] is an inefficient way to give the ball velocity." Also, the depth of heavy spun shots is a lot harder to control. This could lead to many misses if attempting to place the ball too close to the end line, while allowing strong counter attacks if compensating for the lack of placement by backing off the spin or aimed depth.

Fast shot also has its disadvantages. Fast shots taken from the distance decelerate and do not pose a significant threat as the ones taken from closer position near the table. Fast shot with less spin also has a smaller safety margin for clearing the net. In addition, it requires a much improved sense of timing when contacting the ball at a highest point of its bounce.

The good news is that grasping these concepts and gaining valuable experience in the application of speed and spin improves the player's awareness. This knowledge provides a player the tools to intelligently come up with better responses in a table tennis rally.

The Next Step of Development

Warren Spahn, a Baseball Hall of Famer, acknowledged as one of the best pitchers in Major League Baseball history said "Hitting is timing. Pitching is upsetting the timing." This is the soul of many other antagonistic ball sports, including table tennis, especially when the technical foundation has matured for a given player.

The player's job is not simply to win the point. At higher levels of the game a single good play with a serve and a 3rd ball attack is simply not enough to win. One must master to alter elements of technique in a way to remain very consistent and attempt to make the opponent inconsistent. This is exactly where the chapters above come in. They provide the information on how to build your game and gain the understanding in what it takes to create the opportunity for a win.

Why only an opportunity, you might ask? Simple, the games to 11 points are short. When meeting a worthy adversary, it takes only a few mistakes from either player to win or lose the game. Only a few means that for every experienced attacking player, every chance missed to attack is an opportunity lost and every chance taken to attack and gain the initiative is likely a point gained. With experience, especially maturing into a high level player, there is a fine level of a realization that the key to every play is not to blow the ball past the opponent. The key to a great match is maintaining your performance by being able to vary your approach to a given shot. The approach will depend on the tactical opportunities, advantages and disadvantages of a current position. The key is a patient, consistent approach to winning the point.

Table tennis is a game of chess at high speed and to advance farther in the skill level, one needs to be able to produce different responses as solutions to various problems occurring within the rally. For example, many players can only maintain a rally with high speed exchanges, but falter as soon as the rally slows down to slower, spin sensitive counter looping rally. Same can be said about many players that are unable to break themselves out to attack or counter attack after a first block and remain the "wall", until the opponent misses their shot, or they miss their block. What about spin variations? How often have you seen players capable of handling heavy spin with ease only to miss a very basic no-spin ball?

The greatest difficulties in this game are caused not by the faster exchanges, but by variation of the exchanges. The toughest opponents are the ones who are technically strong to produce any type of a shot while you struggle to read the opponent's intent. If this is the type of the opponent that usually is the toughest, why not aim to develop the necessary technical skills in order to become the same, tough opponent?

With these thoughts, the concepts begin to change. Faster speed and power begin to slightly fade away as the number one strengths of a point winning shot. They in turn become the number one elements of finishing shots, but the majority of the points are constructed by patient, well placed shots with variable depth, spin, and speed.

The goals of the service variation, for example, also change. Early on, in lower levels of table tennis, the service variation was used to create opportunities for quick finishing shots, but at a higher level, service variation turns into an opportunity to gain a modest advantage. The goals shift from the ability to set up the kill shot early to the ability of manipulating the opponent to exposing his weakness. This occurs because high level players develop excellent defense. One shot is simply not enough to win. A steady and patient approach is necessary. In this approach, the player freely enters a rally and plays out the point, rather than avoiding exchanges and attempting to score a winner early on.[6]

The next question is whether enough time is spent on a specific type of training that focuses on the awareness of the situation to allow the player to find a proper technical solution to the ever-changing dynamics of the point. Michel Gadal refers to this as "adaptive intelligence." Most players striving to break into the higher competitive levels of table tennis do not acquire sufficient training in this regard. Multi-ball training for speed and consistency is the most common training method, which undoubtedly improves subconscious responses of the player, while strengthening the footwork and physical conditioning at the same time. Generally, however, players rarely focus on shot selection or

---

[6] Incidentally, longer rallies encountered through patient approach also explain why high level players need to spend more on conditioning, cardio, and strength training.

alternatives available to the player at a given moment in a multi-ball drills. Most players use these drills to work their strongest shots.

All of this goes to show that more time needs to be spent on the strategic and tactical foundation of a player's game. How should the player win the points? What are the opportunities that allow the player to quickly take advantage of the point and which require a much more patient approach? The emphasis yet again is on the strong technical foundation and the player's intelligent, purposeful variation of his shots in order to maximize the difficulties for his opponent.

Looking at the game from the perspective of the ever-changing dynamics of the point, the importance of the widely adaptable technique that can be applied to many shots is a much stronger foundation for a growing player. Points are no longer played out by set pieces, but are constructed based upon a much more elaborate analysis of the player's and the opponent's strengths and weaknesses.

All of the abovementioned sections contain the elements of the game as different blocks. However, each player can construct a completely different approach to the game using those blocks. This brings us to the next section of the book, which looks into various approaches that players can use to build their own game by applying the principles of strategy and tactics.

Strategy and Tactics

"In battle, there are not more than two methods of attack - the direct and the indirect; yet these two in combination give rise to an endless series of maneuvers."
- Sun Tzu

Sun Tzu's book "The Art of War" is many centuries old; however his greatest works still accurately reflect many of the aspects of today's societies in many disciplines from military to corporate management, and sports. There are a lot of important thoughts embedded in the pages which are certainly eye openers. The quote below the title of this section accurately reflects the following content. It means that there are many ways to victory. There is no right or wrong way. There is, however, a need to recognize many opportunities that can be utilized in order to gain a small advantage and just as many opportunities to strike to score an immediate small victory. In table tennis, minor advantages yield better chances to win a point and small victories are directly measured as a point wins.

This is not a section that describes generic playing styles and lists a common tactics and strategies to take on an opponent with a certain style. Many other books and articles have already been written on this topic. This material is widely available, but it is far too broad to allow a player to formulate a more refined plan, especially against an unknown opponent.

Let's face it, opponents of a certain prominent style, let's say choppers or traditional penholders are fully aware of their weaknesses due to limitations imposed on them by their equipment, style, or grip. These types of opponents, especially at a higher level, work on the common style related weaknesses to protect themselves from defeat. Yet, even working on style related weaknesses, the weaknesses will still remain, but they have to be properly exploited.

This chapter is dedicated to defining the tactical and strategic principles in table tennis by looking and comparing many examples from other disciplines such as military history and chess. Certainly it's not necessary to have any knowledge of chess or military history to read this chapter. Yet, both of these disciplines represent the oldest forms of tactical and strategic thinking and hence serve an ideal purpose to derive some of the common ideas that suit table tennis as well.

Strategy

"Strategy without tactics is the slowest route to victory. Tactics without strategy is the noise before defeat."
- Sun Tzu

There is a common belief that the best chess players in the world, grandmasters, can count tens or hundreds of moves ahead. This is incorrect. Even the best analytical minds would find that this approach, while feasible, will be slow, difficult, and error prone. This was proven by the very first chess computer programs that were written to play a human being. The notion of calculation quickly became a problem. Forward counting computing algorithms proved to be inefficient to quickly and properly come up with correct moves. Chess players were able to beat the computer quite easily, while the computer was taking longer and longer time to come up with answers to complex positions resulting from human player's moves.

Why were human players able to maintain the upper hand against chess computer programs for a very long time? The answer lies in the ability of a human being to carefully evaluate a given position on a chess board. Positions on a chess board are complex due to many numerous elements. From computer programmers' perspective, the program can only do what it is programmed to do and it cannot "think" outside the box. While the chess programs counted all kinds of variations using the mathematical calculations and iterating through all of the possible moves, a human player was able to quickly eliminate the moves that were not relevant to the existing position and player's strategic plans.

As you can see, the best chess players in the world do not count tens or hundreds of moves forward. The best chess players in the world imagine a position where they have a certain advantage. They set up the pieces on the board in their minds in advantageous way, and then - they count moves *backwards* to figure out *how* to get their pieces to take desired positions! *This* is called strategy.

If you follow military history, many examples of thinking described above will begin to surface as generals of opposing sides choose *where, when,* and *how* they will oppose their enemies using whatever resources that are available at the time. How could the legendary 300 Spartans[7] stand up to thousands of troops? How could Allied forces successfully land on massively fortified Normandy beaches on D-Day? None of these events would have been possible without well planned and executed strategy and these are just some of the examples out of many.

Strategy is envisioning a position which gives you an advantage over your opponent. In military history, strategy is developed by defining *where* and *when* desired battles will take place. Thus, strategy is a plan. Plan full of intelligence and analysis of both side's strengths and weaknesses.

Same rules of strategy also apply for every game that

---

[7] The Battle of Thermopylae, which became legendary due the courageous fight of 300 Spartans, has a lot of various accounts which seem to indicate different sizes of Greek and Persian armies. Depending on which historic sources are references, historians believe that the Greek army consisted of a total of 5,000 to 7,000 troops, out of which 300 were only Spartans, while Persian army is argued to be 70,000-300,000 troops. Nevertheless, 300 Spartans seem to have withstood a significant main offensive for several days, which is impressive regardless whether the Persian army consisted of 70 or 300 thousand troops.

has ever been played. How does a coach set up the players in Basketball, Football, Hockey, Soccer, etc? He looks at player's strengths and evaluates the best use of the player on the field depending on the positions where the players can utilize their greatest strengths. Based on the collaborative strengths of his individual players, the coach is then able to implement a strategic plan for his team to execute on the field. This plan is modified depending on the opposing team's strengths and weaknesses in order to gain a sufficient advantage that will result in a win.

Hence, strategy is not a mere thought that comes up on demand. It is a carefully instrumented plan. This plan, however, cannot be hatched if the player simply does not know his strengths and weaknesses or is unable to properly analyze the opponent to figure out his best and weakest skills. The aspects of strengths and weaknesses are strained over and over in many sports because the most successful plan to victory is found when one party is able to stay away from opponent's strengths and capable to attack opponent's weaknesses.

Strategic Planning

What does it mean to have a plan in terms of strategy? Do you have a plan when you play *all* of your opponents? What is your plan based on? When do you begin to alter your plan? How drastically?

I bet these questions have not been completely answered, let along asked by many table tennis players. It takes a certain type of discipline to approach all of the matches with such a strong strategic focus. Why are so many players reluctant to spend the time to develop their strategic sense, especially knowing that long term benefits of this are undoubtedly worth the effort?

I believe the lack of strategic focus in player's matches is primarily caused by mistakenly confusing tactics and strategy. This is especially true in table tennis where the coach is able to alter the strategic focus of the match from game to game during a break between games. This allows the coach to make some adjustments, but the intervention of the coach for some players seems to lift the burden of responsibility for the overall strategic direction of the match away from the player. Tennis, for example takes a much more thorough approach to strategic knowledge and understanding since the coach is not allowed to interact with the player during the match. These rules force the player to formulate an initial strategy with a coach prior to the match. The rules also dictate that it is the player's responsibility to carry out the strategic plan throughout the match, regardless of the many modifications to the initial plan that will need to be made in the process.

Unable to clearly differentiate tactics and strategy, numerous table tennis players end up executing lots of tactics to win points without a specific strategy. I have heard many players advise their friends and teammates to "mix things up" against a tough opponent. "Mix things up" is not a strategy! What this advice truly does is simply leaves the result of the match in the hands of a more consistent and better prepared player who has a technical foundation to respond to a wider array of opponent's actions than his adversary. Yet, even with an initial strategy that some players try to devise, many players stray from the main plan as the match goes on without even recognizing it and therefore do not capitalize on their opportunities to win.

What does it mean to have a plan then? In table tennis, strategy is defined by deciding what the player will aim to target with his offense or defense. Once the strategy is selected, it is important to stick to the plan without thoughtless deviation.

What does it take to build a strategic plan and maintain its focus during the match? It takes an understanding of various parts of the table tennis playbook, the so called detailed look into the inner game of table tennis. To simplify, let's compare table tennis to with another discipline which requires good strategic fundamentals. Let's compare it to chess.

A chess game is composed of many phases, each having a different purpose and requiring a different evaluation of strengths and weaknesses. The opening is the start of the game where the players aim to develop their pieces in the best way to allow them to take a dominating position on the board. Usually the strategic plans of this phase are aimed to assume a much more dominating position on the board. The middle game is where the players aim to direct their pieces to attack the King. This phase is used to refine the plans in order to maintain the position on the board and oppose the opponent's plans, while allowing the player to build up the strength to attack the opponent's King. The last phase of a chess game is the end game, where players usually end up after a majority of strongest pieces have been exchanged. This phase is very strategic and difficult due to many constraints that exist on the board - shortage of pieces, lack of strengths of attacking pieces, large open space and many unprotected areas as well as time constraints (since chess is played with a clock) and rule constraints (where players must move a piece on their turn and cannot simply take a pass of a next move).

All of these phases require a different strategy because the *purpose* of each phase is conceptually very different. However, all of these phases occur within a single chess match. Where does it fit in table tennis?

Before any of the table tennis players had a chance to serve, the players have a choice to pick their initial match strategy. The player needs to decide how he or she would like to start the match. This is essentially the stage where the player will "develop his pieces." Once the opponent's pieces are developed, the adversary's strengths and weaknesses will become better visible, allowing players to refine their long term strategy and therefore enter the middle game. This is the phase where the opponents will clearly try to target each other's weaknesses and try to utilize their strongest shots. Finally, the players will enter the end game as soon as one of the players will become closer to finishing out a game and a match. These last points in addition to the strategic plan will carry a lot more mental weight and pressure. In table tennis, unlike chess, however, the match is composed of many small battles that are won and lost by points and games, which will give way to many opportunities to reset the match back into an even state.

In chess, moves are either tactical or strategic. Likewise, points in table tennis can be played out with tactical or strategic purpose. A player may choose to win a point by executing a certain tactic based on surprise and variation, or the player may decide to play the point conservatively according to the overall pre-planned strategy. This, however, is determined by the player point to point depending on the player's "feel" of the match, which leaves the player too many choices to be considered to be made in the time between points, and unfortunately makes lots of room for poor choices.

How does one make the right choice instead of the wrong choice? Well, this is where it is important to learn *how* to think.

When I was about fourteen-fifteen years old, I loved playing chess and was constantly beating my friends and family members. My grandmother found me a coach to improve my knowledge of the game so I would continue to maintain my desire to play chess long term. Zakhar Fayvinov was a highly respectable chess master in Saint Petersburg, Russia prior to moving to the US. When we first met and he evaluated my existing chess skills, he told me something that guides my life to this day. He said: "I don't know if I will be capable of teaching you chess, but I will teach you *how* to think."

Our basic lessons for the longest time were not aimed at making me memorize anything. The lessons aimed at my ability to assess a given chess position on the board. He would set up the pieces and ask me questions: "What are the strengths of one side?" "What are the strengths of the other side?" "What kind of strategic goals exist in this position?" "Where are the tactical opportunities in that position?" These main questions barely scraped the surface of the main approach to thinking, which inevitably transposed to something even greater - how to think in life and how to problem solve regardless of the issue at hand.

It turned out that thinking is a lot easier if you know what proper questions to ask. It is even easier to remember these questions, because there are only three!

What do you want to accomplish?

What stands in your way?

How to get around it?

If at any time, there is another problem that is discovered along the way, even during the process of unraveling the details of an existing problem by addressing the question number three above, it is solved exactly same way - by asking the same three questions all over again, but with a different purpose and different level of detail!

This is the basic notion of strategy as well. Strategy is a plan, plan based around the opponent's weakness. All it takes is to recognize the weakness and then ask yourself these magic three questions to figure out how to take advantage of the opponent's weakness and which tools are available at your disposal in order to capitalize on this opportunity. Looking back at the myth of the grandmaster's ability to count the moves forward, one can see the how these magic three questions allow the grandmasters to derive their answers and calculate moves backwards.

This, however, is just skimming the surface of the strategic thinking as there are many other steps needed for a successful strategic plan. For example, how does the grandmaster know which position he should aim to assume in order to gain a decisive advantage? Certainly anyone can envision a position where the opponent is one move away from being in a checkmate, but chances of getting to that position become very slim especially considering a large number of moves that exist to arrive to that position.

This is where the game is broken down to micro plans. Each micro plan seeks to achieve a certain result. Plans are frequently altered along the way because the opponent will resist being manipulated and will hatch a plan of his own, commencing a long term struggle. To be successful, each micro plan needs to be achievable. It is not a good idea to follow the strategy blindly without making adjustments as variables change during the match. Smart opponents will always seek out ways to counter incoming threats.

Yet, having even a poor plan is often a much better alternative to not having a plan altogether. At the very least, a poor plan shows what *does not* work and can be refined to aim at the right weakness in order to make it work. Having no plan means blindly bombarding the opponent with shots at random, which usually means surrendering the initiative and chances of victory to your opponent, especially if the opponent is a stronger player.

The Opening

The match begins with the first opening points. Yet, the strategy must already be planned out by this point. It is quite arrogant to start the match "Gung Ho" and expect to find a way to gain an advantage before the opponent is the first to reach 11 points. This type of a "strategy" is a recipe for disaster. Why force yourself to play catch up even against a weaker opponent? It is crucial to have a plan right from a start.

Strategic choices to starting the match are numerous. One can commence the match with quick, high risk shots to make the opponent scramble and feel rushed or slow patient ones to make the opponent feel slow steady pressure. The main aim at this stage is to utilize the strongest shots against the opponent's weaknesses. Most of the reasoning from deciding how to start out the match will come from the knowledge of the opponent. Against a known opponent whose strengths and weaknesses are better known and understood from prior results, the strategy can be hatched to immediately target previously established flaws, especially if the player has faced his opponent recently as this might not provide enough time for the opponent to sufficiently improve his skills. Against an unknown opponent, a patient and careful "opening" will likely be needed at least until the strengths and weaknesses are better understood and identified.

In chess, for example, there are numerous openings. Many pawns can be moved forward at the start of the game and the pieces can take many different positions to support the advancing pawns as well. Positions that develop by chess openings generally suit the basic character of the player. Some players prefer to play open games with many open areas on the board and quick decisive moves and many fast exchanges. Others prefer a closed position which is full of slow, patient moves resembling movements of boa constrictor, designed to choke the opponent's pieces, carrying the game to victory. This is exactly how the "mood" of the table tennis match also gets created. Some players will want to be the ones to control the tempo and the initiative of the match, since this is where they ultimately shine, while others might prefer to respond to the tempo imposed by the opponent. The strongest battles usually rage where both parties fight to retain their own initiative on the table.

The most interesting aspect of chess openings is that very few players deviate from their usual openings. Most of the players have certain specific openings, depending on whether they play the white side or the black side at the time. The reason for it is that they would like to play the game in such a way where they have the upper hand in terms of knowledge of various positions they can strive to achieve by executing a given opening. This means that every player has a plan in mind in how they will most likely attack the King from the position that they originally set up on the board.

How do the players know where to set up their pieces before the chess match develops into a full battle?

This is where the theory behind chess becomes very important and knowledge of the many combinations in the chess openings becomes irreplaceable. Essentially, the concepts are documented by many world class players who have written a ton of books on many openings and the historical matches that have been played out by grandmasters over the years. In addition to the knowledge of theory which guides the moves in the openings, many generic principles must be followed by the player in order to successfully finish the opening and transition into a middle game.

    Table tennis has a similar way to conduct such openings. They revolve around the concepts of "set pieces." Service and the 3rd ball, for example, are the main set pieces that make up a table tennis player's arsenal. The players know which serves produce the type of service returns from the opponent that will complement their attacks. These are essentially the grounds of the table tennis openings. Similarly to chess, table tennis players will prefer to open or play out their points with either long, or short serves depending on their preference and comfort level. The opponent's will also resist each other's openings with service returns that again yield a much more favorable opponent's response, in order to completely prevent or simply oppose the opponent's attack.

    Thus, each player will begin the match with their usual, comfortable and thoroughly practiced routine or set of routines depending on the favorable variation that the player prefers to execute. Depending on how these set pieces play out, subsequent strategic goals will be modified to attack the weaker parts of the opponent's game with the strongest possible weapon available at the player's disposal.

Types of Strategy

There are only two types of strategy that exists - defensive and offensive. While many players train a large variation of strokes - both defensive and offensive, only one type of strategy can be executed at a time. Attempting to build the strategy by constantly modifying the strategic focus no longer makes it a strategy. Instead this type of variation results in a match consisting of only tactical combinations and has limited application with a much reduced effectiveness.

Where most players lose themselves is trying to classify themselves as attackers or defenders in terms of style or the type of strokes that they prefer to execute, while in reality the greater majority of the players execute a defensive strategy. This does not mean to retreat every time a player is attacked or to be constantly under opponent's pressure by only utilizing a block, chop, or lob. The goal of defensive strategy is to outlast the opponent in the rally by placing one more ball on the table than the opponent is capable to attack. The focus of this strategy is to win by patience and attrition through control and consistency regardless of the type of shots that will be used to return the ball. The players utilizing this strategy can initiate their own attacks, but they only do so when the opportunity presents itself to do so, which is usually following a weak return.

Offensive strategy is executed when the goal of the player is to put the opponent under pressure by continuous attacks, aiming to score points with consecutive powerful shots despite the type of responses produced by the opponent. This strategy aims to always score the points by being the one to put the ball away. The issue, however, is that this is a very risky strategy. When the player constantly attempts to put the ball away by placing it near the edges and driving the ball with more power, the errors become easier to make. Therefore, consistent attacking shots against various types of responses are necessary in order to make this strategy effective. Otherwise, if the player is constantly missing, this strategy becomes more like a timer for self destruction. A typical example of this is visible in a thriving junior player who has great strokes but poor shot selection, frequently losing the matches to opponents with clearly weaker skills. The opponent does not counter attack, but despite strong attacks by the junior player, they aim to only put the ball back on the table. Strangely enough when these players meet for a match, this strategy succeeds more often than not.

Strategies are picked depending not only on the player's preferences, but also by many of the player's assets such as speed, power, footwork, defense, consistency, patience, etc. Amateur players, however, as noted by Allen Fox frequently make wrong strategic choices. "In my experience the most common strategic mistake made by recreational players is attempting to be attacking players when they only have the tools to be defensive players." These players attempt to hit too hard and too soon resulting in many unforced errors, not realizing that they are not being beaten by the opponent, but instead, are beating themselves.

Experienced high level attackers, for example, recognize when it is best for them to utilize a defensive strategy rather than an all out attacking one. When two table tennis attackers of the same skill level play each other, the one to attack first is usually the winner of the point. The reason for it is that their set pieces, the serve and attack, at this level allow them to initiate their fully planned attack, while the opponent's defense is usually a notch level lower. Unable to suppress the opponent's attacks or defend them consistently, these players compete with the tools they have. The victory of the match usually goes to the player who makes fewer mistakes throughout the match. This is what we call "anyone's game." Both players are equally capable of winning. However, when the same players play a higher level attacker, the higher level attacker has an easier time beating his less experienced counterparts by utilizing a defensive strategy through control and consistency, while being able to put away a loose ball when needed. The reason this strategy works against a lower level player is that a lower level player generally attempts to take higher risks against a higher level opponent. A higher level opponent on the other hand is capable to oppose an attack with the skills of attrition and defense, prompting the lower level player to take even more risks.

This consequently demonstrates that successful defensive strategy means committing to returning every single point over and over as long as the play requires. Meanwhile, offensive strategy means setting up the point in a way to score a quick victory with a violent blow and continuing high intensity attack as long as it is necessary, until the rally ends. Neither of these strategies rely on the first, second, third, fourth or fifth ball in the rally. These strategies are long term plans, which patiently set and maintain the rhythm of the match.

How does one know if the strategy is working? "Most players don't realize their strategic shortcomings… As long as the player can't hit the ball in the court more than three, four times per point, this does not become an obvious problem if the opponent can't either…" said Allen Fox. This is a very basic fundamental that explains how strategy separates players of many different levels. Lower level players do not build their game around strategy since they are not consistent enough to target a strategic weakness, while upon further improvement strategic plan becomes a vital part of the match in order to find a way to defeat even the strongest opponents, but it is important to have the technical foundation to maintain the rally long enough to gain a required advantage.

In his book, Allen Fox provides an example of attacker's strategic ineffectiveness during the match where an attacker faces a so called "dinker" in tennis. The same type of player can be found in table tennis. A player who is less orthodox, frequently less aggressive, but much more patient and strategic, often using alternative rubber covering such as pips or anti. This type of a player proves to every opponent that his attacking strategy is not working by demonstrating how he is ready and capable to return dozens of attacker's shots, while attacker misses his shot a lot more frequently by attempting to blast the ball past his "easy" adversary. "For every player who thinks he is capable of hitting his shots hard and near the lines, the dinker simply shows him he cannot." Hence, all loathe towards the cheating ways of anti, pip blockers and choppers in table tennis. Most players have a hard time facing a harsh reality that their game is not strong enough to play a high risk game and still win against a so-called "player with no skill." Players that struggle against "dinkers" express disgust to face similar style players in the future. In reality, these matches would be a lot simpler with a well planned strategy aimed to patiently exploit a certain opponent's weakness prior to moving in for a final blow.

We now arrive to a very basic insight of the game. It turns out that the number one skill in table tennis is not a single shot such as the forehand loop. It is the ability to keep the ball on the table! This yields our focus back to the first section of the book. Consistency and control are the main weapons, which are produced by reliable strokes. The speed, power, and placement of the shot are built on top of the consistency. The strategy used, hence, depends on the ability of the player to accurately and consistently produce desired shots when the opportunity exists. This is achieved with technique. Otherwise, without the proper tools and especially using the wrong strategy, the player will leave himself exposed to defeat a whole lot sooner.

The next question is whether the strokes or technique are what guides the strategy or does the strategy guides the developments of the strokes and the underlying technique? There is no definite answer to this question as both can be instrumented after the other. Yet, this is a very important question for coaches that initially draft the future of their players. Most coaches would agree that there is yet another type of strategy that exists in table tennis. It revolves around the concept of strategic player development. How exactly does a coach create an ideal player? What to teach him first and what to add later?

The basic dilemma is whether the coach would rather teach the player to play or teach the player to win at the current phase of the player's development. The general knowledge and understanding of the principles of strategy is enough to construct the training and match play in accordance to the player's capabilities. The key, however, is to compete within one's potential in terms of technical skills and strategic guidance. This is the best recipe for steady improvement and long term success.

Strategic Approach

There are two types of a strategic approach – direct and indirect. Direct approach is seen mostly at the lower level of table tennis because the weaknesses are very obvious. For example, players that do not have a good enough backhand can be directly attacked in their backhand zone for a quick and easy victory. Even if the shot is returned every once in a while, percentage table tennis will prove that the attacks into the backhand zone of this type of opponent over time will be sufficient to win the match, especially if the opponent does not exploit his adversary's own similarly severe weakness.

Direct approach is very obvious and can be understood and opposed with simple solutions, especially if the opponent does not modify his strategic plan. In an example above, a player with a weaker backhand may choose to step around to cover his backhand with his forehand in order to minimize the effects of the opponent's exploitation of the weakness. Another alternative is to change the placement of the ball so that the rally would lead to a forehand to forehand exchange. Yet, this is too visible, too simple, and too easy. Higher level table tennis requires a much more elaborate approach not only because the weaknesses are less obvious, but also because the strengths are much more severe.

Indirect approach is a lot more cunning as it involves

a much deeper analysis of the opponent's technical flaws[8]. This is where we can utilize centuries worth of strategic knowledge from military history.

Sir Henry Liddell Hart, a leading military historian and theorist of the twentieth century simplified many aspects of military strategy to the basic principles of indirect approach with the following statements:

- **direct attacks against an enemy firmly in position almost never work and should never be attempted**
- **to defeat the enemy one must first upset his equilibrium, which is not accomplished by the main attack, but must be done before the main attack can succeed**

Sir Liddell Hart studied many of the great military figures, such as Napoleon, Balisarius, and especially the works of Sun Tzu. These commander's battles proved that indirect strategic approach to attack is the best possible way to be ready to address a dynamic environment on the battlefield. He specifically pointed out that a strategy based on "elastic defense" accurately satisfies the guidelines of the indirect approach. His works demonstrated that it is a far more superior strategy comparing to the rigid strategy around powerful direct mass attacks or fixed massively fortified defensive positions. Sir Liddell Hart's view was yet again proven by Erwin Rommel's African campaigns during

---

[8] The warm-up in table tennis is a good point to try to understand how the opponent approaches his shots and where he can be set off balance in terms of timing, especially in lower levels of table tennis.

World War II.

These strategic fundamentals directly apply to table tennis. Indirect strategic approach is the core of the high level table tennis. This is exactly what is referred to as "knowledge of how to construct the point."

Direct approach loses its effectiveness as the player's level begins to climb and his improvement launches the player to compete with more experienced adversaries. This type of a swift climb through the "ranks" leads to many problems and plateaus for an improving player simply because the player does not realize or understand that the strategic approach to the match needs to be completely different. An elaborate strategic plan needs to be devised to compete at the higher level, unlike the previous matches the player has played in the past. Continuously attempting to win the same point by directly attacking an opponent's "weakness", as the player has been used to doing, only yields to quicker losses. It is no longer enough to attack a *ready* opponent and expect to apply the type of pressure needed for a win.

Military history provides great examples of defensive strength of fixed positions against direct attacks. The 300 Spartans were ready to defend an extremely large army and successfully suppressed it's advancement for several days. Meanwhile, D-Day invasion of Allied Forces during WWII was planned specifically in a way to avoid attempting to breach intensively fortified static defenses especially after the failure suffered at Dieppe Raid[9]. Against a well defended adversary, the strategy calls for an indirect approach, first step of which is the aim to loosen the opponent's defense by purposeful maneuvers.

The "elastic defense" principle or the indirect plan fits perfectly with the defensive and offensive type of strategic focus in high level table tennis. This principle applies as the ability of the player to keep the ball on the table using defensive strategy through attrition while seeking out opportunities to tactically score a victory. In simple terms, playing the rally in a way that would be safe and consistent while fighting for positional advantage where the opponent will lose his balance and provide an opportunity to win the following point.

Looking at the way we play the matches, we now understand the concepts behind the very basic principles of exchanges in table tennis. On a slow ball, it is best to respond with a fast shot; on a fast ball, it is best to respond with a slow shot; on a medium pace ball, it is best to respond with the medium pace. These principles are in accordance with the defensive and offensive strategic plans. Fast shot is used when the opponent produces a slower and usually easier shot to attack. When attacked with a fast shot, it's best to defend with control and slow down the attack and when receiving a controlled shot, it is best to try to control it back in an attempt to attain a superior position. For this reason

---

[9] The Dieppe Raid was a major operation designed to test out military capabilities of Allied forces by attacking the German forces at French port Dieppe. The plan was to conduct a simple "Hit and Run" attack of the port, but it underestimated the defensive capabilities of the German forces. The initial plans included using paratroopers to take out German Batteries covering the sea, but the plan was altered to be a fully sea landing operation. The direct assault from the sea was executed on August 12, 1942 with disastrous consequences and enormous casualties.

the player either aims to either win by attrition through consistency or attacks with a final blow if the opportunity is there. Otherwise, one is simply maneuvering for advantage.

An example of a player violating the principles of exchange is often seen by the results of quite a number of matches where lower level players play against higher level players. Lower level players frequently say the following words after yet another losing match "the opponent really didn't do much, but I lost." What do these words imply?

The best way to describe these words is with yet another one of Sun Tzu's quotes: "All men can see these tactics whereby I conquer, but what none can see is the strategy out of which victory is evolved." In the heat of the match, it is very hard to decipher the opponent's plans. Table tennis is not chess and the positions keep quickly changing in every shot and every point. The tactics are more visible since they can be identified by the successful or failed final shot of the rally. Yet, strategy remains hidden, especially if it is based on an indirect approach.

How can a player recognize the opponent's plans? Brad Gilbert provides insight into his approach to decipher opponent's plans through his magic question "Who does what to whom?" If a player continually looks at the points being played out as if he is a spectator, hints at opponent's strategic plans will begin to surface. However, the player does not have the same type of perception on the court since strategies and tactics are recognized better from a third person view. A coach on the sidelines is a very important resource for a table tennis player, the one that can help the player to fine tune the effectiveness of his strategy by observing the match and altering player's approach.

If the main strategy is based on the ability of a player to remain consistent and seeking out opportunities to finish out the point, why do the professional table tennis players hit the ball so hard most of the time and are successful at winning their matches?

Professional players train to compete in this type of a strong, competitive environment. Their shots look incredibly strong for amateurs, whereas comparing them with the rest of their arsenal of their point winning shots they are not absolute winners but rather an extremely high quality consistent, sustainable exchanges. After all, they work on various parts of the game including maximizing the power of their shots by constantly trying to increase their physical strengths. Hence, their shots are strong, but reasonably consistent. Yet, most of the professional player's focus still aims to achieve superiority by gaining a positional advantage prior to capitalizing on it to win the point, even when it looks as if they are slugging away at the ball with all of their might.

Look carefully within the list of top professional players in the world and you will find that while many of the players have strong attacking strokes and are stylistically classified as attackers, only a fraction of these players seem to build their game around a direct attacking strategy. The most interesting observation of the top player's game is identifying the exact instance when these world class players decide to defend or control the point, rather than go for a win. The ultimate struggle in a match is that fine line between control, risk, and opportunity. It takes patience, it takes understanding of the game, and it takes high level skill to be able to incorporate this in in the next step of your game.

The Middle Game

Let's backtrack to the strategic example of chess, where the middle game identifies the time when the game reaches the climax of the battle. This is the same stage as the pinnacle of the table tennis match. Usually this occurs when sufficient knowledge exists to correct the strategic focus of the match. The question here is how and when does the player adapt and maintain his strategy to be more effective.

Imagine a match where you have a chance to score some points based upon an initial strategy, scoring an initial lead of 4 points. Then all of a sudden, the opponent begins to catch up. This happens slowly, but surely. Score first becomes 4-2; then 5-3, then eventually 5-5. What is actually happening? Is the strategy working or not?

The most interesting aspect is the dynamics of the score and how the score plays a part in the result of the game, match, and strategy. The game can start out rather slowly for some players, but careful tweaking of the strategy will allow the player to recover the lost initiative and get back in the game. By the same token, changing the strategic focus without a need can also allow the player with the lead to falter instead. The score plays a vital part in the match. Too frequently the strategy is changed by the player *because* of the score, rather than an actual threat from the opponent.

Some players need a longer time to warm-up and play their best. Although this fact needs to be properly addressed by the coach and the player as soon as possible, this does happen quite often. Thus, the initial lead that looks so promising has not really showed which part of the strategy is or isn't working, especially considering the first game. Yet, when the opponent begins to recover the deficit, does the strategy need to be changed or not?

In order to understand this question, let's look at the dynamics of the match where two attackers are playing each other. Players alternate serves and each of the players will attempt to execute his or her own strategy. Therefore, the serving player generally will try to be on an offensive, while the receiving player will likely be on a defensive. It's not possible to execute both defensive and offensive strategies at the same time, so each player will have to respond to the opponent's initiative primarily depending on whose turn it is to serve[10]. Prior to altering the strategy, it is important to realize what exactly is happening on the court. Is it a strategy that needs changing, or merely a response to a given serve?

Often, one of the players, even with a good initial strategy, will begin to respond to the opponent's actions, giving up the initiative and beginning to alter his own strategy instead of merely altering their approach to a given shot. In the heat of the match, our minds get consumed and

---

[10] Service return is one of the most difficult skills in table tennis, hence on return of serve it is best to commence a defensive strategy, keep the ball in play and simply try to neutralize an opponent's attack, rather than aim to win the point. This long term strategy has much more significant success on the outcome, rather than an aggressive offensive service return strategy aimed to score the point. Offensive strategy only works against easy simple serves, most likely delivered by a much weaker opponent.

we are not always able to think quickly and clearly to realize our next steps. Hence, the players need to take the time between points and assess their game plan. The three questions for strategic plan need to be asked. What is your goal? What stands in your way? How to get around it?

The middle game will consist of a lot of maneuvering. The more severe the opponent's weakness will be exploited, the more it will become visible what is exactly is being exploited and the sooner a smart opponent will begin to work around the weakness. The opponent will attempt to find a proper solution to his weakness, adjustment of which may take a few points or less, depending on the opponent's skill.

Once the match reaches a score of 7 for one of the players, the players will enter the end game.

The End Game

Brad Gilbert, author of "Winning Ugly," became a successful tennis player because he properly identified strategic advantages and opportunities that exist in tennis and learned how to capitalize on them. Score wise, for example, Brad Gilbert emphasized the importance of being the first to get to a score of 30. For him, this was a crucial position. At 30, the player has a chance to apply an immediate pressure on the opponent by getting to 40 on a next point. The opponent, however, needs to score two points in order to end up in the same position! In table tennis, I believe it is vital for the player to be the first to end up with a score of 7. This is where the end game of the table tennis begins.

Why 7 instead of 8 or 9, or even 10? Consider finding yourself trailing when the opponent gets to a score of 8, 9, or 10. You will certainly realize that you are quite late to be able to manage the next few points well, especially if you need to make a strategic adjustment. The odds are not in your favor by quite a margin. Pressure sets in and thoughts of tactical combinations to quickly score the next few points begin to creep in.[11]

---

[11] This is exactly where players begin to stray from their strategic plans, constantly trying to catch up by attempting to get a chance to execute an easy kills shot after a surprise serve.

Table tennis is highly unpredictable with many of the opponent's tactical strengths based around strong serves. They can do a lot of damage, yet, even a mere net or edge ball will be enough for the opponent to take a decisive advantage or a victory. The secret, therefore, lies in being able to manage the game and the match with smallest risks possible, a principle of getting farther by going slower. Since the hardest thing in table tennis is to consistently maintain concentration throughout the match, if you find yourself focusing a little harder on the last few points of the game earlier than your opponent, you will reach your ultimate peak of concentration at the most crucial time!

There are a few other reasons why 7th point is highly important. Think about the scoring system overall. At 6-6, the player who gains the next point has a very strong position. If the player serves at 6-6 and wins the point, the player can take a further lead to 8-6, or remain in neutral at 7-7 on the opponent's serve. Allowing the opponent to win the next two points will be disadvantageous, so this is where the concentration must peak. With 9-7 lead, the opponent is two points closer to victory, while player is four points away. Even if the player exchanges the next two points by splitting 1-1, the opponent still has a much better advantage with 10-8 lead and his serve. However, if the player recovers the deficit of two points and takes the game to 9-9, the opponent has a disadvantage of returning the serve. Therefore, the player who is serving at 6-6 needs to work extra hard to secure the next two points to gain a better position in the game with better chances for victory.

By the same token, if a player is receiving at 6-6, it is best to play in a way to at least ensure a solid position of 7-7 with his serve coming up next and the same dynamics as described above. Falling behind at this point in the game with a score of 6-8 and an opponent's serve coming up means that the chances of winning the match stack up significantly against the odds. Therefore, it is important to put all of the effort into making those 7s count in order to prevent the opponent to assuming a dominant position.

What does the score have to do with strategy? As in chess, the end game is very delicate. Aside from staying on top of strategic plans, the main emphasis of reaching the end game is that the adjustments to strategy need to take place prior to arriving to this phase. Attempting to make adjustments at this phase means taking risks which may not pay off due to the extremely crucial phase of the game and the match. It takes only a single mistake to trigger a shift in a momentum in order to secure victory or suffer a defeat.

The key to a good strategic plan is envisioning a position where you have better chances to win. Let's say you play a strong opponent whose techniques are much stronger. This player is fast and consistent, but you figure out that this player does not play with the same aggression when he ends up at 9-9 or a deuce. This player plays a very passive safe game at this point in a match instead of the solid attacking one. In this scenario, it is important to put all the effort into maintaining a balance of points and end up with a score of 9-9, where the opponent has a slighter weaker game. The main question to ask yourself is "what would allow me to win?" The aim is to put all the effort to assume the next attainable position "If I score the next two points, I think I can win." It's not a guarantee of a result, but the effort and belief that victory is possible is often enough to work harder at the crucial moments to improve the chances for success.

The end game is also the stage where tactics based on quick exchanges aimed to rapidly win a point, such as a 3rd ball attack, come with a burden of pressure and may not prove to be as effective for some players. Although it depends on how the player is capable to perform under pressure, most players would find that the end game is best played out with solid strategic focus, despite the players strengths of serve an attack. At a higher level, experienced opponents already acquire a good amount of knowledge and experience against many serves that have been executed prior and will unlikely be caught unprepared to return. Trying out a new serve may prove to be a gamble against some opponents as well since the opponent may be able to handle that specific serve with ease, while hurrying and forcing to take stronger shots means taking more risks of placing the ball into the net or more often off the end of the table.

I think most players would agree that while the entire match and every game can be extremely difficult against some opponents, the last few points generally are the hardest ones to win. The end game does not forgive rashness or carelessness and the best way to deal with rashness or carelessness is by having a proper, carefully devised strategic plan on how to exploit the opponent's weaknesses with maximum control and lowest amount of risk.

Innovation

I know what you're thinking. It must be a typo. Why is the section on innovation embedded into the chapter on strategy? I assure you it is not a mistake.

Table tennis is a discipline like many others. The sport constantly undergoes many changes which impact the way players play the game, and the way they prepare and develop those fundamentals. Techniques of the game taught a decade ago were a lot different from the elements that are taught now. Techniques of tomorrow will change as well. The principles of speed and spin will remain the same, but the importance of those elements changes.

These changes occur for many reasons. Equipment rules, game rules, and other regulations certainly play a part in introducing changes, but there are also strategic ones. If we look at the history, we can see how European hardbat play was defeated by Asian quick attack style. The pip out quick attack style was defeated with a stronger spin of inverted rubber. The spin oriented game was defeated by powerful quick off the bounce forehand game. Now the powerful forehand attacking game seems to be defeated by a dominant backhand play.

The sport is constantly undergoing changes. The reason why this is important in the context of strategy is that there is a strong relationship between a given technique and the strategy.

All techniques in table tennis have a strong side and a weak side. Hence, the top players in the world are constantly searching for new techniques that can be used as the antidotes to the superior strengths of their peers. 2013 World Table Tennis Championships in Paris displayed a new emerging development in table tennis. Dominant backhand and forehand play is beginning to be challenged by a very consistent blocking game. Attacking players cannot ultimately execute powerful shots all the time, every time, and will have to execute a control shot to recover when they overextend themselves. This is where this new blocking game provides on opportunity for the player to go on the counter offensive.

There are several reasons for this development. First and major one is that all players have different strengths and cannot play the same way. Even if we were always able to copy world #1, we would forever be on the end of the innovation cycle. Just as another player is training to copy of the strengths of the world #1, another player emerges on a scene with a new set of strength that are able to neutralize current champion's strengths.

Another reason for this development is that innovation occurs as a strategic effort by planning on establishing a different strength to challenge an opponent's strengths a lot sooner than this type of a game publically emerges in the world competition arena.

Some of the prominent examples are the developed technique on reverse penhold backhand[12] and the European backhand. Reverse penhold backhand was responsible for reviving the style by resisting strategic weaknesses of penhold players, while European backhand, once identified as the weakness of the European game, was adopted and developed to an even higher degree to be regarded as an even greater strength in modern play.

Innovation is a result of experience. It is a result of a problem – solution paradigm. The best way to achieve innovation in table tennis is by understanding potential opposition's training. If you know what is currently "hot" in table tennis techniques and can figure out a method to avoid those techniques or how to defeat them, and especially if you train the skills necessary to withstand them, you are strategically better prepared to challenge them.

Those that strive to be victorious need to embrace discovery and innovation. In the words of late Steve Jobs, "Innovation distinguishes between a leader and a follower."

---

[12] Traditionally penhold players used one side of the paddle in play and were quite limited in the backhand zone. Reverse penhold backhand is a penhold technique of executing a shot with the back side of the paddle. It practically eliminated the backhand as penholder's weakness.

Developing Strategic Sense

There is no curriculum for developing a good strategic sense. Formal education of it does not exist. Although some coaches try to raise the player's strategic awareness, most coaches do so only in matches, rather than spend the time preparing the player for a certain strategic direction off the court. This type of training frequently seems to take a spot behind further stroke and footwork development. Therefore, most the strategic knowledge is gained through experience.

Mark Twain said a very important quote "Good judgment comes from experience. Experience comes from bad judgment." Like anything that is learned by experience, developing a strategic sense becomes a trial and error process. Yet, it does not have to be this way. Most of the knowledge already exists. It rests comfortably behind the foundation of technique. Do you recall the initial discussion whether technique guides strategic development or whether the strategic development guides the technique? In the aspects of this chapter, strategic sense is developed with the technical capabilities.

Think about all the elements that go into a table tennis stroke - spin, speed, and placement. All of these elements can be changed and all of these elements produce a certain different behavior of the ball and hence require a different approach to the next shot. Spin quantity can be changed; so can the speed of the shot. Placement can be changed to vary depth, height, and direction. All of these elements combined together can be altered to produce a different type of shot for your opponent to handle. The shot does not always have to be a blistering one. It can be a cunning no spin flick, or a slow, deep loop. A chop can be loaded with spin first and then have absolutely no spin, requiring a different timing point and approach. Any element can be changed to alter the speed, time, and angle prompting a different technical response from the opponent.

The skill of strategic sense lies within the foundation of technique, where a player is able to purposefully change the various elements and the intensity of those elements on demand, rather than produce the same identical response. This is what it means to develop a solid strategic sense.

The quote by Sun Tzu explains what it means to have a have a sound plan: "If your enemy is secure at all points, be prepared for him. If he is in superior strength, evade him. If your opponent is temperamental, seek to irritate him. Pretend to be weak, that he may grow arrogant. If he is taking his ease, give him no rest. If his forces are united, separate them. If sovereign and subject are in accord, put division between them. Attack him where he is unprepared, appear where you are not expected."

The thoughts of the quote are based upon the principle of imposing the type of a game on the opponent that forces him to play out of his element, away from his strengths. The more uncomfortable the opponent is, the more risks he will take and the more mistakes he will make in the progress.

Let's take Allen Fox's "dinker" as an example and set the stage for his match against a typical attacker. The attacker seeks fast shots, but "dinker" gives him slow stuff. The attacker wants spin, but "dinker" gives him none. The attacker wants easy, high pop up service returns, but the "dinker" gives him low returns of different depth. This type of a match completely takes the offensive player out of his element, where he is unable to use his usual strengths. This is the "dinker's" strategy and the offensive player just got suckered into playing the type of match he does not want to play.

Now let the tables turn. We pick an attacker who does not object to his opponent's preference to slow the game down and is patient, consistently returning the ball on the table until he has a clear chance to win the point. The "dinker" wants fast incoming shots, but this player gives him slow spin. The "dinker" wants his opponent to rush by attempting to score a winner sooner, but instead gets patient returns. This is the type of the game that "dinker" does not want to play and now we get the opposite result.

As you can see, a successful strategy means giving your opponent the type of the game where he cannot engage all of his strengths and cannot create the type of a tempo and initiative that allows his game to flourish. Eventually, taking all opponents' strengths away leads to the total surrender.

What if the "dinker" all of a sudden makes an adjustment against a patient opponent and begins to attack? Well, now we have a match that will depend upon the way each player will be able to sustain the rally and the victory will go the more consistent player capable to better handle his opponent's game. At this point, however, it becomes important for each player to know his or her weaknesses and be prepared for the opponents to find them and attempt to exploit them. Yet again, we come back to the training hall and begin to look into the training necessary for the long term strategic development of the player's skills, where the most prepared player who knows his strengths and weaknesses is usually the better player.

Tactics

> "Strategy requires thought. Tactics require observation."
> - Max Euwe

If you ask a player to define table tennis tactics, most players begin by providing examples with a sequence of shot combinations. For example, "I played that player and I gave him this serve and he returned it to my forehand and I attacked down the line." While this sentence does describe the scenario and the shot exchange, it really does not define the tactic. Tactics are much more complex and require a deeper understanding than just a one, two shot combination.

Tactics are present in every single shot exchange. However, there is a significant difference in an observer perceiving tactics from the sidelines by noting which player executed what kind of shot and when, versus the player purposefully executing a given tactic because he was capable of recognizing and taking advantage of an opportunity.

So what is truly a tactic and how does it differ from strategy? If strategy is planned by identifying *where* and *when* to attack or defend, tactics are identified by answering the question of *how* to set up the desired strategic play.

Max Euwe in a quote above said it best. Strategy requires upfront thought and plan. Tactics is the ability to capitalize on an opportunity. Certainly every shot allows for opportunities, but what will separate a good player from a better player is that a better player can recognize when the play calls for a tactical combination and be able to choose the *right* combination to gain an advantage. The better player can also approach desired tactics with very little shot making risks, while the less experienced counterpart will likely take too many unnecessary risks too early.

Here is a simple example of a play that involves both strategy and tactics. One player determines that his opponent has a weaker push and a soft block on the backhand, but a very fierce counter on the forehand. Strategically, this player then decides that the best way to play his adversary is to force him to push a ball and then attack his backhand. This strategy would force the opponent to block the ball softly and in turn allow the player to gain an advantage of the soft block to attack the next ball with a stronger shot, such as a power loop. This type of a strategic play can be set up on player's serve using a short underspin serve, or it can be forced upon the opponent on his serve by returning his serve short.

Certainly, the opponent might not serve the type of a shot to allow for a short return, so this scenario will need to be evaluated as well, but for the sake of the example, let's assume that the opponent always serves in a way that allows the player to return the ball short. Over time, this strategy will make it clear for the opponent that he will be beaten unless he tries to vary his responses and work around his weaknesses. One of the options for the opponent is to try to try to avoid using a soft backhand block and instead use the strong forehand. However, this type of a response will open the room for many tactical combinations. How the opponent will move in order to attack the shot and where he will aim to place the ball is what will define the tactical opportunities for the player.

This section is specifically dedicated to defining and providing examples of tactical combinations. These combinations will fulfill the player's arsenal of choices, which in the long run develops the player's intelligent problem solving abilities.

Tactical Awareness

There are many materials that provide examples of tactics. Yet, I find that most of the materials list the information in a very inefficient form. "If he does this, you do that. If he does that, you do this" seems to teach a very programmatic or robotic tactical response. Besides, with so many players playing the game differently and having different skill sets, can you truly expect the player to remember all of the tactics in such a list?

Let's go back and review the proper ways to think and look into such a programmatic example. It is apparent that this example teaches the player a possible action, but does not teach a player how to properly construct a tactical combination. Simply put, such examples do not provide an answer to the very first question of thinking - what is the player trying to achieve? What is the goal?

Player's goal obviously is to win the point, but within the rally, there are different ways to capitalize on every opportunity. The more tactically aware is the player, the more ways he can approach an opportunity in the point. The game is too fast to think, but having even a small, well defined tactical library of combinations opens up many choices with much better chances to win. The missing link is the training aimed at maximizing tactical awareness. This training improves player's ability to recognize when tactical opportunities arise as well as ensuring consistent shot making in a tactical combination.

With these thoughts, we arrive to understand the basic principles of tactical awareness. Tactical awareness is knowing *what* every tactical combination aims to accomplish. *The purpose* is of the most vital importance. The purpose derives the best application and with application comes experience. The only limiting factor of the player's tactical abilities is the size of the player's tactical vault - exactly how many tactical combinations does the player know that can allow him to gain an upper hand in the match. Granted the player is capable of consistently producing the shots necessary to execute the tactical combination (and hence again the importance of technique), the player will be capable of making adjustments in order to influence an outcome of the match or at the least to put up a stronger resistance to his adversary.

Tactics play a vital part in higher levels of table tennis because the top player's techniques are solid enough to withstand any direct attacks, especially when evaluating percentages of player's shot making abilities throughout the match. Hence, strategies formulate around tactical combinations. Top level players have no immediate weaknesses, so the matches are structured not around a weakness per se, but around the openings or opportunities to win the point. The success of the match often depends on the player's ability to create such opportunities - which is what tactics aim to achieve.

Principles of Tactics

Tactics and strategy emerged from many centuries of warfare. Different fighting methods and weapons have been created and adopted by various fighters, and with experience, the warriors have discovered that every weapon has some advantages and disadvantages. Thus, there were many ways to combat someone and the type of the approach to combat had a direct impact on the outcome of the battle.

Consider it similar to "paper, rock and scissors" game. Each one defeats the other. Therefore, it is very important to make a proper choice in the selection of a weapon in the military history example. Thus, tactics became the fundamental methods for engaging and defeating the enemy in battle.[13]

Historically, what made things even more complicated in military was the creation of military units of various different sizes and the emerging combined forces doctrines. The commanders of military units realized that they were unable to battle every enemy identically because of various strengths of opposing forces. Therefore, many different types of forces were introduced into the armies to improve upon an army's capabilities - archers, cavalry, foot

---

[13] I hesitated to use the word "techniques" here in place of "methods" in order not to confuse the table tennis technique, which obviously has a different meaning. However it is best to substitute "methods" for "techniques" for readers that will not get confused with that statement.

soldiers, elephants, phalanx, and many, many more. Each type of forces added to the mix allowed significantly more tactical choices over how to achieve a desired victory. Yet, even with the increased number of variations, the tactics primarily aimed to satisfy principles of a maneuver.

There are several basic principles of a maneuver. One is changing your own position in order to attack the opposition's weakness. Another is to force opponent's movement to occur, which would expose a weakness.

The opponent is forced to maneuver when visible threats are recognized. If the threat is strong enough, the adversary has to move to negate the threat or else suffer a vicious blow.

In the military, units are composed of a certain limited number of troops and resources. Therefore, when the enemy is responding to a threat, it is forced to weaken some part of its force. For example, a military unit racing forward to catch a retrieving army will stretch its communications and supplies and will have difficulties in acquiring reinforcements and assuming defensive positions if needed. A military unit changing the direction of attack or defense to fend off an attack from one flank will expose himself to a possible flank attack from a different direction and will be overrun if the enemy has plenty of forces to attack both sides simultaneously. Thus, maneuvering plays a vital part in being able to force opponent's responses in a way to lead to victory, especially if the opponent is not able to fully negate the threats with the current position and resources.

There are many different types of maneuvers available at a general's disposal. One of the most common maneuvers has already been mentioned above. It is the concept of flanking. Flanking is the action of circumventing opponent's primary forces in order to attack an undefended side of opponent's army where the opponent will become overwhelmed and incapable of producing a strong resistance. In history, successful flanking maneuver always had a significant impact on the battlefield. However, it is impossible to flank the opponent with a primary force.

Consider two boxers in the ring. Both are aware of each other and while each of them would definitely want to flank the other with a hook or a side step and punch, they both "dance" in a circle in preparation of each other's shots. However, flanking can be successfully done using a relatively weak punch called a jab. Jab suppresses the opponent's actions for a slight second and allows the fighter to attempt to create an opportunity of utilizing the flanking movement and a punch from a different direction.

The very principles of military maneuvers that follow the guidelines of suppression and flanking are the elements that have a direct relationship to the concepts underlying positional tactics in table tennis. Certainly, there are other types of tactics that exist in table tennis. Those are covered in further chapters. Yet, positional tactics in table tennis are the most important types of tactics. As the level of the player goes up, tactics of deception, spin variation, service, and service return will only be marginally effective against technically strong, experienced players. Meanwhile, the importance of positional tactics goes up as the player's level climbs.

Tactical Approach

Placement is one of the most important tactical elements in table tennis. When the placement and direction of the ball changes, the opponent must move in order to return the shot. Even though a table tennis table is only five feet wide, it is impossible to effectively defend all of the space without movement. Once the player moves to cover a threat, he leaves another area of the table unprotected and vulnerable to a follow up attack. [14]

Therefore, there are two ways of scoring a point in table tennis. One way is to attack the opponent directly and have the opponent miss the shot. Another way is to attack the open space of the table, forcing the opponent to move to get to the ball.

Hence, we have two basic elements - the so called pin, and the switch. The pin is similar to that of chess, where a piece cannot be moved because it would open up the attack of another higher value piece or a King located on the same line of attack. In this example, the player is the pinned piece that cannot move. His position is locked in a spot that

---

[14] This is exactly why footwork development maintains a high level of importance in a list of necessary table tennis skills. The player has to be able to move effectively to cover the initially created placement and move back to cover the prior occupied position. It is also important to learn the shots to force the opponent to move farther so that the opponent is unable to easily return to recuperate from a prior shot.

is consistently being attacked by strong shots. The player simply cannot move fast enough in order to allow himself to get out of the way safely without taking risks of losing the next point. The best alternative for a pinned player is to

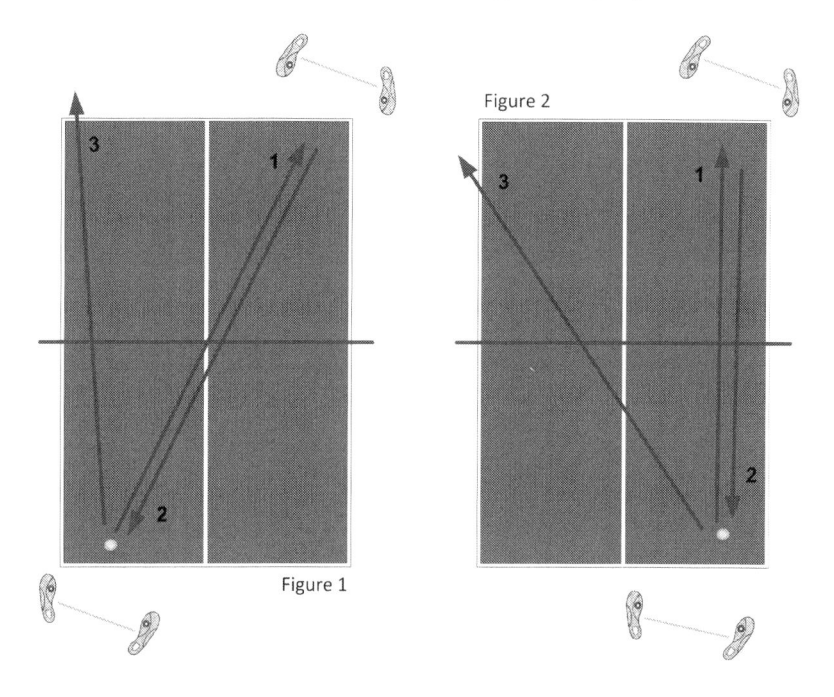

Figure 2

Figure 1

Figure 1 shows that the player on the bottom of the picture can first directly attack opponent's backhand in order to lock the opponent in place. That is generally achieved with a threatening, high quality shot identified by arrow 1. The opponent will most likely simply bring the ball back. Since most threatening shots will come back into the same area of the table where the original shot was created, the player is likely to receive a ball back as demonstrated by arrow number 2. At this position, the player can attack open space as demonstrated by arrow 3.

Figure 2 shows similar position as Figure 1, only identifying an attack down the line. This position however will be less likely occurring for a right hander player for two reasons. First, it is generally easier to execute shot number 1 cross court than down the line. Second, even if the shot number 1 is executed down the line, opponent's most likely response will be backhand block cross court. However, if the player is left-handed as the feet position suggests, then the scenario demonstrated in a diagram is very likely to occur. Shot at arrow 3 again, identifies player's tactical opportunity to attack the open space.

defend, especially if the attacks are strong enough to maintain the pressure. Because the player is unable to move, it makes his actions very predictable which is what opens up the opportunity to exploit the pin with a tactical switch.

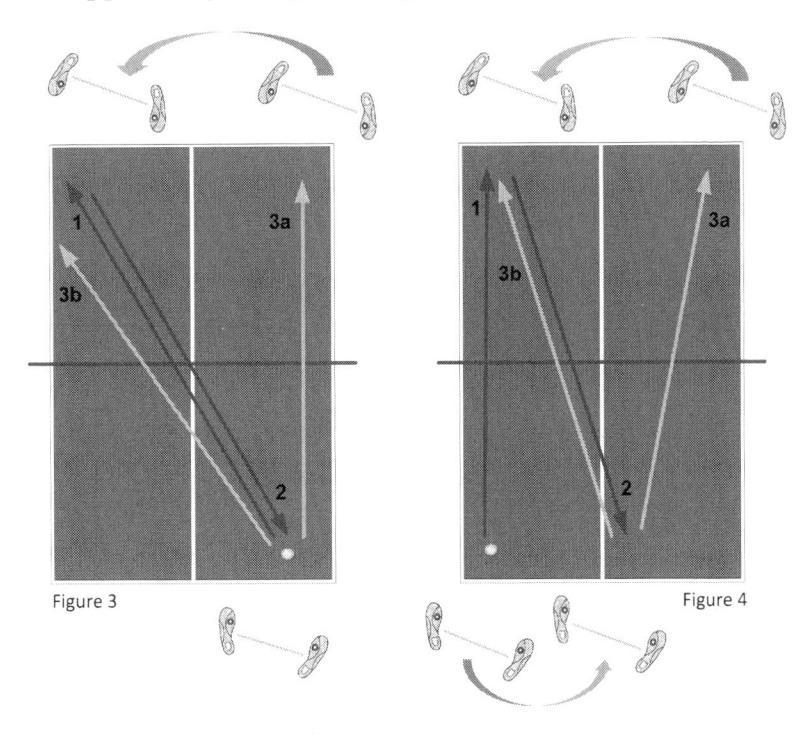

Figure 3

Figure 4

Figure 3 and 4 demonstrate the player on the bottom first attacking opponent's wide forehand and then having a choice on shot selection at arrow 3a or 3b whether to attack the same spot or the newly opened spot of the table. The opponent has to consider the threat of the open area being attacked, so he can be wrong footed if attacked back in the same zone, especially if his response to shot at arrow 1 is weak. Please note the difference in responses of the opponent to the initial attack. If the opponent is able to reach the ball in Figure 4, the player will have to move. If the player is late, the ball will likely be placed into the middle of the table, which is a poor placement. Shots placed into the middle of the table in a desperate attempt to simply keep the point alive, will usually be attacked even stronger.

The switch is the principle of switching direction of the next shot by placing the ball away from the opponent, forcing the opponent to ultimately run to defend the shot.[15] At the highest level, most combinations in table tennis are composed using both of the principles. One way is by first pinning the opponent from being able to effectively commence the movement and then attacking the open area when the opponent finally produces an easier shot as displayed in Figure 1 and 2.

The other alternative is to attack the open space of the table first, forcing the player to move and then deciding whether to attack previously occupied, but now open area of the table, or yet again, send the ball directly into the opponent (Figure 3 and 4).

A generic concept of application of pin and switch is demonstrated in Figure 5. The examples provided above are simple, yet, there are numerous approaches to achieving both the pin and the switch that are very specific to table tennis. Table tennis is a very complex game because a player can utilize speed and spin to add another level of complexity for the opponent. Not only can the player attack the opponent using placement, but the player can also vary the quality of the attacking shot and hence change the ball's behavior. Suddenly, directional attacks can be slow or fast, which in turn will vary the distance the opponent has to travel to the ball and direct attacks can be varied to deliver

---

[15] Going back to the prior section of the book that looks at the control element in table tennis, forced movement and hitting the ball on the run strains the technique to its maximum and makes many players incapable of continually producing good responses, hence becoming an effective way to set up winning points.

different quantities of speed and spin where even a prepared, experienced opponent can make a mistake. Finally, tactics can be even more effective by utilizing deception which is designed to disguise the player's intention from the opponent and catching him by surprise.

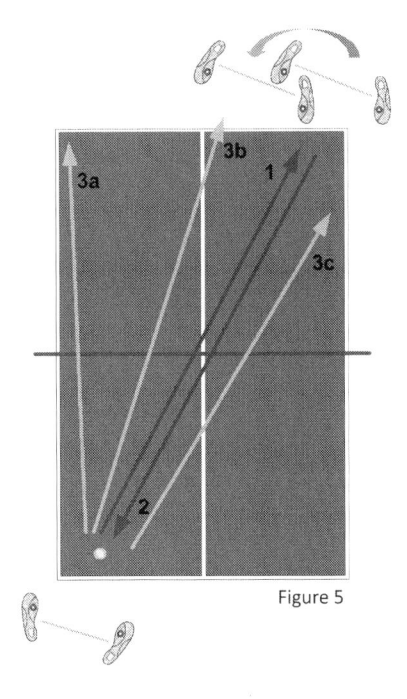

Figure 5

Figure 5 shows options of player at the bottom of the diagram after a return of an initial shot or a pin. Arrow 3a shows example of attacking open space, arrow 3b attacks the point of indecision referred to as the hip or the elbow. Arrow 3c demonstrates an attack of a spot prior occupied by the player. The key to knowing where to attack lies in trying to understand what kind of a shot the opponent believes he needs to defend. The pin, however, will likely only occur with a series of exchanges of shots identified by arrows 1 and 2. Otherwise, it is fairly easy for opponent to achieve movement after one shot, as opposed to locking the opponent in one position for several shots. In this scenario, the player whose techniques are not deceptive will find that the opponent will recognize easily when he needs to move in to cover attack in the arrow 3a. This is where attacking the middle will be a better option. For players who over-anticipate attack of 3a, it is best to target spot identified by arrow 3c.

The tactical approaches to winning the point are numerous, especially for an experienced player with good technique. All of this information boils down to the way a player can utilize a certain table tennis shot in order to gain an advantage. Intermediate table tennis players have a tendency to block the ball passively, for example. While their defense of the shot is relatively consistent, the problem occurs immediately as the opponent is able to attack the blocked ball hard in the opposite direction on the next shot. This example demonstrates that the pin is achieved with spin by producing a spiny opening and it sets up the next shot for a switch.

When the opponent blocks the ball very well or counters with some pace, the point will depend on both of the player's ability to sustain a quick exchange with control, especially whenever the direction of the ball slightly changes. Coincidentally, the pinned opponent can also switch the line of play on a weaker shot as the means to unpin him or herself, however that is generally riskier than maintaining a quick counter. This is demonstrated in Figure 6.

In Figure 6, the players keep exchanging shots back and forth to each other, designated by arrows 1 and 2. Yet, when the opponent is ready, he can attempt to step aside and change the direction of the shot as a way to unpin himself. The new position, however, is slightly problematic for the player at the top of the diagram. We will cover this a little bit later.

Figure 6

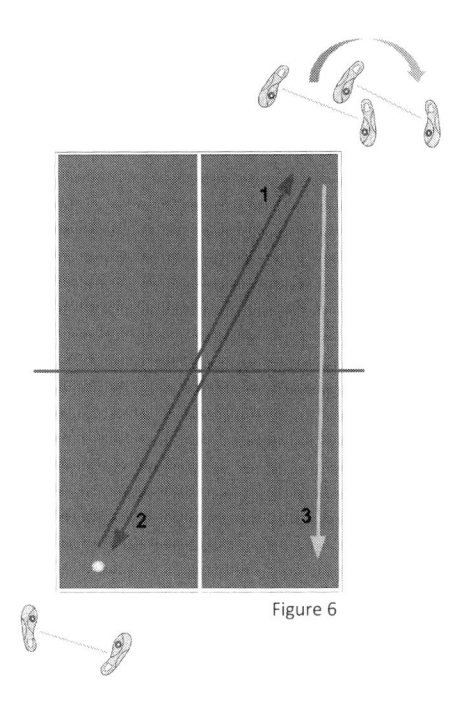

Figure 6 shows how the opponent can unpin himself by being the first to execute a switch and change the direction of the ball.

How does the player use speed in a tactical combination? Shouldn't the player attack with maximum speed and maximum control at all times? Yes, absolutely, however the use of speed tactically is somewhat of a misnomer. Speed by itself does not win the point. What does win the point is that the higher speed takes the time away from the opponent. This time is necessary to mount a proper defense. Without sufficient time, defense breaks down. In this context, the tactics are based more on time rather than speed. The best of example of this is a tactic on exploiting an opponent who prefers to play farther off the table. On a shorter shot, the opponent has to come in closer to the table and if his shot is not adequately strong, the point can be won by attacking the ball quickly before the opponent has the ability to retreat to his comfortable position away from the table.

The best example of deception in tactics occurs during service and service return. These skills have a completely different set of attributes allowing the player to set up strong attacks such as spin variation, depth, speed, and placement. Yet, when the service is well executed and the contact point between the ball and the paddle is well hidden by the player's motion, it usually leads to an immediate point. Same goes for a well executed service return.

Looking at various tactical approach examples, it seems that every single point played on the court is composed of a tactical combination. This is certainly true. The only question regarding this fact is whether the player executed a tactical combination consciously, subconsciously, or luckily. The ability to "automatically" being able to evaluate opponent's position or movement during a rally and recognize which shots are available at player's disposal directly contributes to the player's skill level.

The good news is that tactical skills can be developed. The player with the best tactical awareness is the one whose training specifically aims to develop the tactical patterns necessary for the player's game. Tactical training teaches numerous tactical approaches to various shots, opponent's position, and opponent's responses.

If we were to reverse Brad Gilbert's quote on reading the game - "Who does what to whom?" in a player's first person, we get "What do I want to do to the opponent?" It is important to know the answer to this question upfront instead of asking and deciding the answer to this question at the same time as the ball is traveling from the opponent's paddle and begins to hint an opportunity to execute a tactic.

Tactical Geometry

If in high school I was told that I would again need to use geometry I would probably never believed it. Yet, I find myself thinking in term of geometric positions a lot more in table tennis, especially when evaluating positional advantages and tactical opportunities.

Table tennis is not a precise science, but geometry is. Player's footwork can be evaluated for efficiency merely by drawing a geometric picture produced by both of the player's positions and movements on the court. Geometric figures drawn from player's positions allow calculating the best areas of attack even against a player that has smooth and excellent movement because the point in the rally continues well beyond a single tactical switch. Yet, several directional switches in the row are usually enough to force the opponent to lose balance, slow down his movements, or simply lose a point in an error.[16]

The basics of tactical geometry are guided by biomechanical differences between forehand and backhand executions. Forehand technique and the footwork toward the forehand naturally allows the player a much wider reach. Forehand technique is a lot more flexible in terms of timing too. The player has many timing points along the

---

[16] This is the reason why most points in table tennis are won in 3-5 shots. Tactical combinations based on deception and strengths of the opening shots are key contributors of the ability to quickly create and capitalize on given opportunities.

ball's trajectory that can be used to comfortably return the ball. The ball can be attacked strong even when it has traveled past the optimal contact zone, which is ideally located in front of the player. Some of the late timed shots are usually of a defensive nature, but even they can be executed in control when reaching or moving to the ball. As the player begins to move wide to the forehand and begins to transition his arm towards the backswing position, he naturally creates extra energy to the movement in the direction of the ball. This minor detail has very significant impact on the overall mobility of the player and player's forehand shot effectiveness.

On the backhand side, the window of opportunity to produce a quality return is a lot smaller. The player has to be well positioned in front of the path of the ball in order to execute a sound response. Wide shots in the backhand zone, especially when executed on the move, are usually very passive only aimed to place the ball back on the table. Offensive shots from such position are pretty much a gamble. Various players have occasionally been able to execute a fantastic shot by attacking a slightly wider ball to the backhand. This shot is risky and statistically impractical. For some backhand dominant players, late timed and slightly wider shots from the backhand become consistent signature shots, yet for the majority of traditional forehand dominant players, the weakness around the backhand area, especially farther from the table, requires a much more elaborate focus on the footwork and recovery by ensuring the player's position is perfectly aligned to take a backhand ball in front of the player, at an earliest possible timing point.

Figure 7 Figure 8

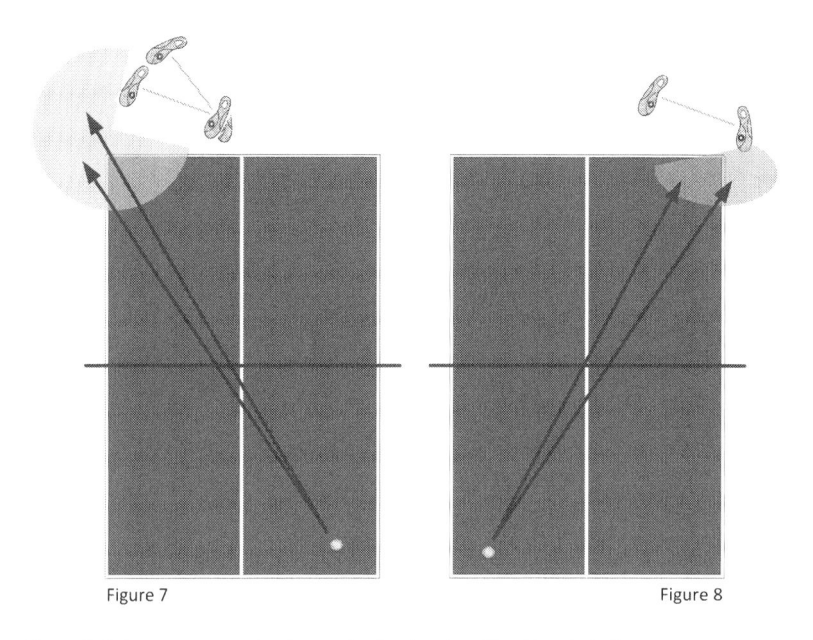

Figure 7, 8 demonstrate optimal areas for forehand and backhand playing zones

Figure 7 and 8 demonstrate the areas of the player's reach on the forehand and the backhand zones. The forehand allows many positional alternatives for the player and hence the ability of the player to take the ball in many various points along the bounce of the ball – on the rise, peak, or descent. On the backhand, however, the area of ball contact should be in front of the player or ever so slightly lower – at the hip, however, the window when the player can take the ball closer to the hip is extremely small and any attempt on taking the ball later to the side of the player is extremely risky (hence players choose to roll or lob the ball back on the table from that zone).

Figure 9

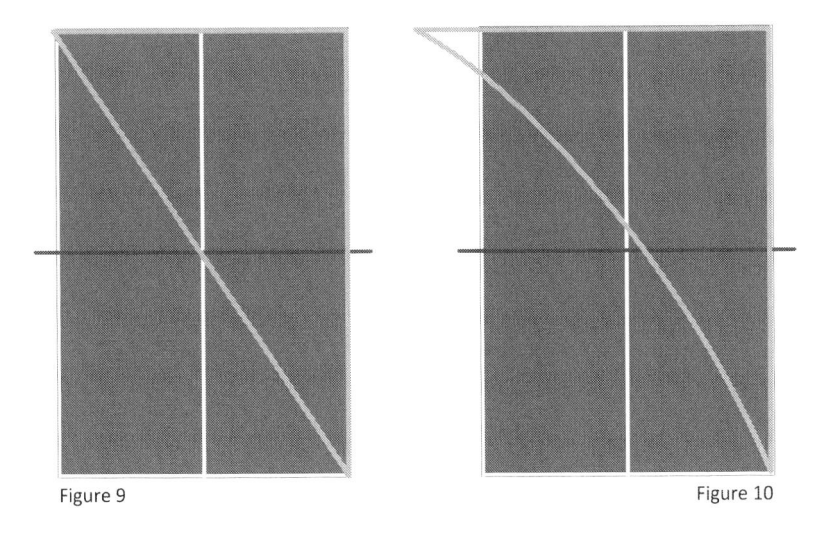

Figure 10

Figure 9, 10 shows how sidespin can be used to change the distance demands for a player by curving the ball a lot wider.

Let's now look at some basic geometric models. Figure 9, demonstrates a very basic picture of a triangle drawn over the table. The basics of that picture shows that the shortest distance between a backhand and forehand corner is down the line, while the longest distance is cross court. However, this is only partially true. Advance sidespin techniques shown in Figure 10 allow bending of the lines to occur, which skew the lines of the triangle a lot more and make footwork and movement a lot more difficult.

Comparing these two figures, it is easy to see a significant difference in the triangles that can be created with an element of sidespin. Thus, demands of the player's footwork are increased with much more pronounced sidespin. The good news is that sidespin ball will be a lot slower than pure topspin because its energy is split between top and side rotation as opposed to only topspin rotation. Hence, the player can still reach a wide ball, especially if he recognizes opponent's intentions early.

What happens when we begin to draw out several different diagrams by varying the initial position of the opponent? During the match, opponent's position constantly changes and it is important for every player to understand his own movement and his own preferences of the attacking zones, so that it is a lot simpler to come up with a proper tactical shot when the opportunity presents itself.

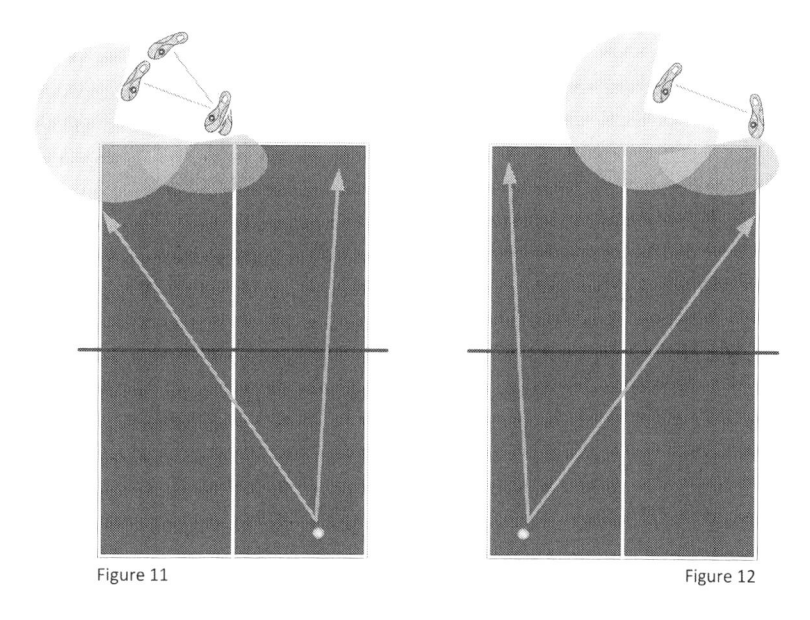

Figure 11

Figure 12

Figure 11, 12 show zones around an opponent which are most suitable for attack since they will avoid the areas where opponent's forehand and backhand can be used. These zones will require the player to move in order to negate the threats. The zones are small, so precision is more important rather than power and speed. This picture does not demonstrate another option – crossover point or the point of indecision (elbow or the hip) because it is a moving target making it hard to achieve accurate placement.

As you can see in Figure 11, the change of the initial position identifies new best areas of attack, which are optimal to continue to apply pressure on the opponent. Coincidentally the diagrams again display that the best shots are not always the powerful, blistering ones, but are the ones with a fine precision and as much strength as necessary to apply pressure on the opponent to make him use proper technique to return the shot.

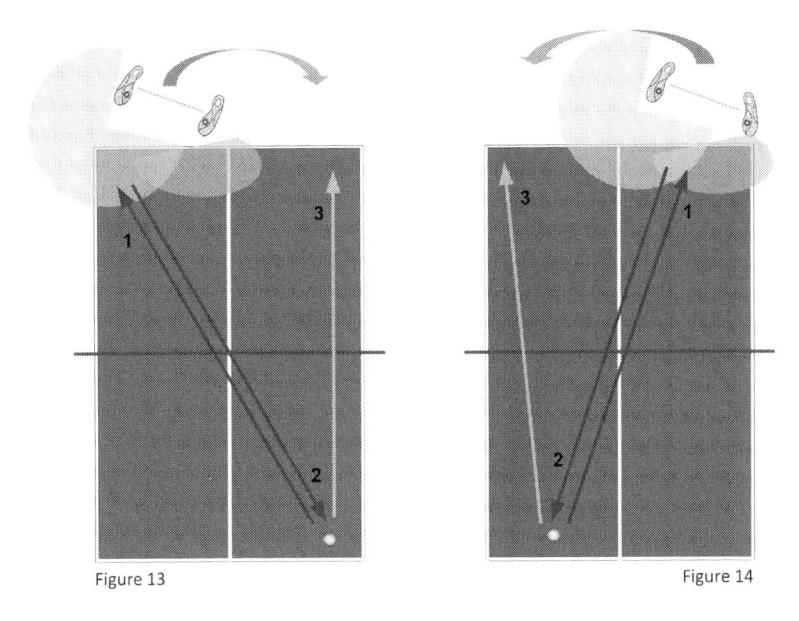

Figure 13

Figure 14

Figure 13 The player is forced to return a shot to a wide forehand identified by arrow 1. The player had to move into the wide forehand to return the shot, but moving into that position, he exposed backhand zone, which is attacked by the player demonstrated by arrow 3.

Figure 14 The player is attacked directly into the backhand. When the player is attacked in the backhand from the middle of the table, it is hard to find a proper placement to return the ball since the opponent is within comfortable reaching distance for most shots in that placement zone. Hence, the option is to put the ball back to the opponent in order to minimize player's own movement upon the next shot. This is where the opponent can try to attack the ball wide to the forehand as demonstrated by arrow 3.

Figures 13 and 14 show some optimal tactical diagrams frequently used at high level table tennis. The patterns are quite simple, but they are the basic of most of the exchanges.

Diagram in Figure 13 displays a player who has to respond to a wide forehand ball and then is forced to return an easier ball that is placed to the backhand. This tactics aims to first move the player wide, and then challenges the player's footwork and his ability to adequately return the ball to the backhand, which is perfect for challenging players with only one strong wing such as traditional penholders and forehand dominant players. It also works against choppers that have a weaker forehand. This tactic creates an opportunity to score the point after the backhand shot is returned. If an attempt is made to win the point with a shot to the backhand, the advantage of the tactic is not fully realized especially if the attacking shot is missed most of the time. This shot is a lot harder than it looks on paper. It takes patience and experience to resist blasting the ball in the opposite direction. Often, putting extra pace on the shot to the backhand in this tactic also allows the opponent to return the shot with more ease because it can be sufficient to simply redirect the ball. A slower, spiny ball is a lot harder to deal with, especially on the run.

There is a small, unspoken secret in table tennis – if you produce a technically strong shot (one that has good combination of speed and spin), it will take technically strong response in order to return it. Thus, every effort must be made to continuously produce strong, technical shots especially during tactical combinations because again, the aim of the tactic is to setup a winning environment. The player who attempts to take advantage of the first possible opportunity without patience is taking more risks rather than following through to realize full benefits of the tactic.

Diagram in Figure 14 demonstrates a different tactic where the player is first forced to respond to a direct attack to the backhand and aiming to switch the line of play on the opponent's backhand return. This tactic is good against players with weaker backhands and slow or inconsistent forehand pivots around the backhand. Players with strong forehand pivots around their backhand are often very comfortable executing a weaker backhand shot because it lures their opponent into attempting to attack their backhand again and this is where they pivot to counter attack the incoming ball. In higher levels, this tactic is only marginally successful because players do not have immediate weaknesses and are comfortably controlling openings to their backhand, but are also extremely quick at pivoting on that shot for a counter attack. Therefore this tactic, at the higher level, is achieved by continuously delivering strong, fast shots to the opponents backhand in order to freeze the opponent's movement and pin him in one spot before attempting to change the direction. Yet, this takes a much more refined level of skill to execute with success. Nevertheless, this is yet another set of tactics available at player's disposal.

These two basic tactical combinations evolve new tactical opportunities. As the match goes on, both players will begin to respond better to the tactics by beginning to anticipate opponent's intentions. The nature of tactics is that they are positional and opportunistic. Hence, when one player will attempt to position himself better for a possible tactic, he will open up another opportunity that can be exploited by another tactic.

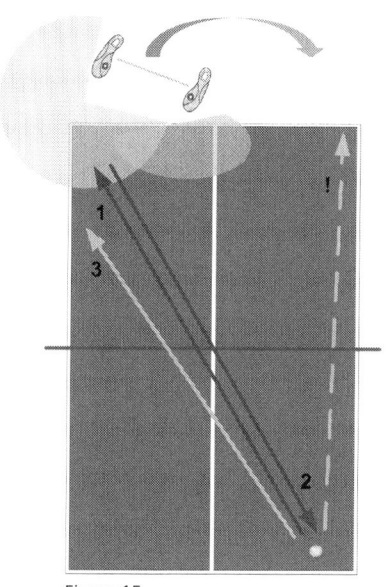

Figure 15

Figure 15 The player returns a shot marked by arrow 1. He had to move into the wide forehand to return the shot, but moving into that position, he exposed backhand zone. The threatening shot is marked by a dashed arrow with an exclamation mark. The player aims to hurry to the backhand, but is attacked again in the same spot in the forehand shown with arrow 3. If the player over-anticipated the threat and initiated the move earlier than the opponent shown the intention, the player will be wrong-footed and will likely lose a point.

Looking at the first tactical combination of first moving the player far to the forehand and then producing a shot to the backhand, if the opponent adjusts and is able to get to the backhand and begin to produce stronger responses, a possible tactical opportunity exists by threating to place the ball into the backhand, but then change the direction of the shot and put the ball back into the forehand zone, as shown in the next diagram in Figure 15. The opponent attempts to respond to the threat by beginning his movement to the backhand a lot sooner, but he might misread opponent's intentions. This is called over-anticipation, which often exists in lower level because of recurring and repetitive training routines. Players begin to respond to familiar placements instead of reading the opponent's shots. [17]

One position that has not yet been covered revolves around understanding the importance or rather volatility of the middle of the table. Consider the following diagram in Figure 16. This diagram shows one very significant observation. Changing the line of play from the middle of an opponent who originated the shot to the middle does not create any tactical advantages. As a matter of fact, the player can choose other placements quickly and easily from those positions as the movement is not difficult. In this position, it is best to attack a crossover point.

As you can see in the diagrams, there are many plays and alternatives and it is important to understand player's positional advantages and disadvantages in order to properly select a tactic that a play calls for – a tactic that is not risk averse, but rather patiently deliberate in creating opportunities and maintaining a consistent pressure on the

---

[17] Coincidentally this is where it is important not to fall in love with a specific drill or training routine. Training routines need to constantly change to target various placement zones and moving patterns.

opponent by forcing him to play on the upper limit of his skills and abilities.

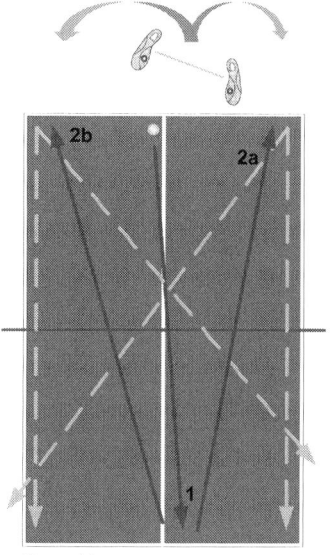

Figure 16

Figure 16 demonstrates that a player who originates the shot into the middle is within a comfort zone for both backhand and forehand response on a subsequent shot to the corners. The angles for the opponent are minimized for shots taken from the middle. Hence, if the ball produced by arrow 1 into the middle that is returned into the corners of the triangle (arrows 2a & 2b), this placement presents no significant threats for the player. In addition, the player gains a shot selection advantage by having a wide array of placement options identified by dashed arrows. This position is very delicate and needs to be well understood in regarding to maintaining the initiative and deciding proper placement.

A proper way of capitalizing on the tactics is by maintaining an initiative and pressure on the opponent long enough to either get an easy shot or force the opponent to falter in an attempt to come up with a proper response.

Placement

Tactics have a single very important requirement – ability to control placement. It makes it very ineffective to attempt a tactic when a player does not have an ability to put the ball in a proper zone and with a proper direction. However, even when the placement is well controlled as a skill, it takes a whole new dimension to be able to properly select the placement during the exchange. Even at the higher levels, players make mistakes selecting a proper placement for their shots. Unfortunately, those mistakes have severe consequences and players are punished for those mistakes with unnecessary losses. Let's look at some examples and identify some of the most common mistakes players make.

Below are three diagrams displayed in Figures 17-19 where a player makes a set of placement mistakes. All of the shots demonstrated by the diagrams indicate that executing this type of a shot makes it easy for the opponent to find and target a different placement zone for a counter attack.

In Figure 17, the player on the bottom of the diagram can place his next shot to a forehand corner and force player at the top of the diagram to move in order to cover the distance. After the player at the bottom executes his shot, he will also begin to move further to the middle of the table in order to minimize the angles that his opponent can gain if he is able to reach the returned shot.

The problem with the placement selected in this picture is that the player minimizes the severity of the shot by attacking his opponent directly without stretching or forcing significant movement. In addition, the player will be forced to cover more ground on opponent's shot, while the opponent's initial movement will be a lot shorter.

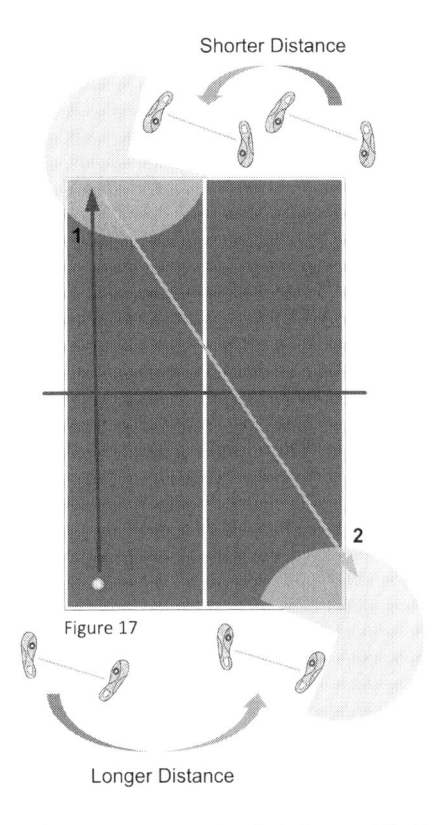

Figure 17

Figure 17 shows how players can erroneously select placement that is easy for opponent to respond to, while inadvertently creating a position where subsequent movement will be significantly more difficult.

The only time a player can be effective with that shot is if his opponent does not have adequate defense skills or time to mount a defense, if the quality of the attacking shot is extremely powerful in terms of speed and spin, or if the ball is placed directly into the crossover point or point of indecision of the opponent.

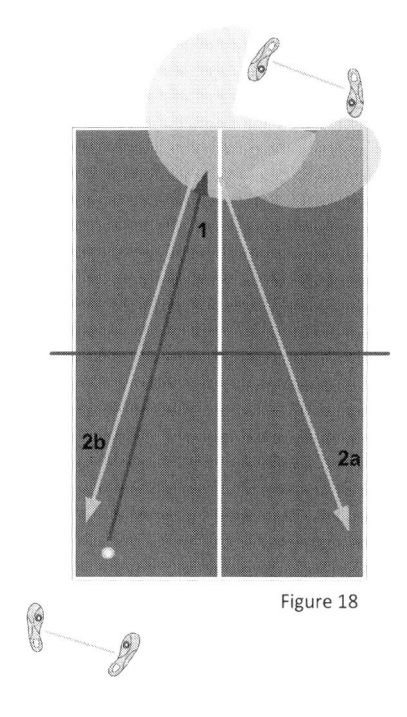

Figure 18

Figure 18 demonstrates poor choice of placing the ball into the middle. This shot often happens when attempting to target opponent's middle, but making a mistake with accuracy. The opponent has a lot of good choices for his next shot and can take them with comfort since the ball is placed right into an optimal stroke zone.

The next diagram on Figure 18 illustrates player A returning the ball to the middle of the table. The middle of the table is a very delicate spot, as it was mentioned in prior chapters. It is effective to play a ball into the middle of the table only when it is possible to place the ball into that spot accurately. When the opponent is moving across the middle attempting to reach the other side in order to negate a thread of a wider ball, it is usually a good time to place the ball into the middle. However, in the scenario shown on the diagram, the player places the shot directly into his opponent's stroke and will likely face a strong shot wide to his forehand or wider to the backhand. Without forcing movement, opponent's shots will also be a lot easier and less risky.

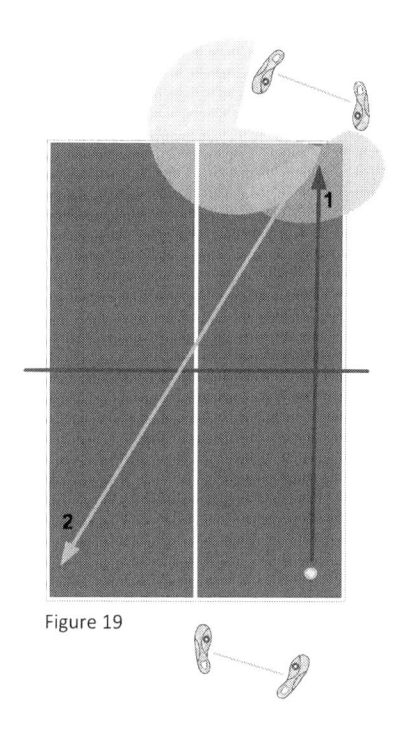

Figure 19

Figure 19 shows an example of attacking opponent's mounted defence, when the opponent is ready to defend without any movement. If the player's attack is not adequately strong, the player will likely lose a in this position. Hence, down the line shots are best utilized as point winners.

In the third example shown in Figure 19, the player attacks the ball down the line, while his opponent can simply block the ball wide to the backhand without having to work hard to gain the advantage. This is an example of attacking a mounted defense. Unless the player's shot is a very strong one that can go "through" the opponent, it will put the player under pressure if it is returned into the backhand zone.

These diagrams demonstrate how placement plays an incredibly important part of the game. Certainly, shots can be of various strengths and the player can win points attacking even the areas shows in the diagram with success, however then, the points are won by the strength of the shot and not by proper application of tactics. If two players of the same skill level play each other and one player consistently places the ball in a wrong zone, chances are that the player making the least number of tactical mistakes will emerge a winner.

If the diagrams above demonstrate the mistakes, what are the proper placement zones in the same diagrams? Before we begin to review the proper placement, let's trace back to the beginning of the chapter that describes the tactic. Each tactic must have a goal, a purpose.

What kind of a tactic can a player set up from his position in Figure 17? If the player is able to quickly pivot and execute the shot faster, he can certainly loop down the line with success. It is also possible to produce a little sidespin. Yet, aiming to place the ball too close to the lines is quite risky. Even with the best placement, a mere cross court block, if the opponent can get to the bally will be enough to counteract this shot. Instead, it is a lot better and less risky to place the ball slightly wider to the opponent's backhand as demonstrated in Figure 20. When the ball goes wider to the backhand, the opponent will be unable to pivot with ease and will have to use his backhand.

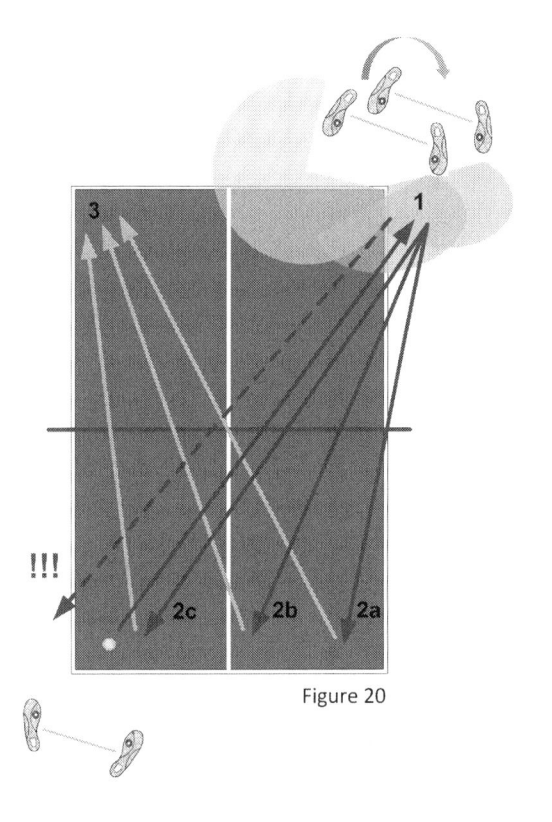

Figure 20

Figure 20 shows a very busy diagram where opponent's responses are noted as arrows 2a, 2b, and 2c. The best opponent's response is identified by the dashed arrow with exclamation marks. All others yield imminent attack of the open space marked with arrow location 3 when the opponent is forced to take a step further into the backhand corner to defend a shot to a wide backhand.

To execute a good backhand shot, the opponent has to move slightly farther to the backhand. Because the opponent ends up wider from his backhand corner on the next shot, his backhand down the line block or counter is a lot harder to achieve, but also any placement to the forehand zone, or the middle of the table will allow the player to score the point by going wide to the forehand. Opponent's safe response is therefore limited to attempting to return the ball even wider to the backhand of the opponent, but this is an extremely difficult shot both in terms of placement and in terms of control.

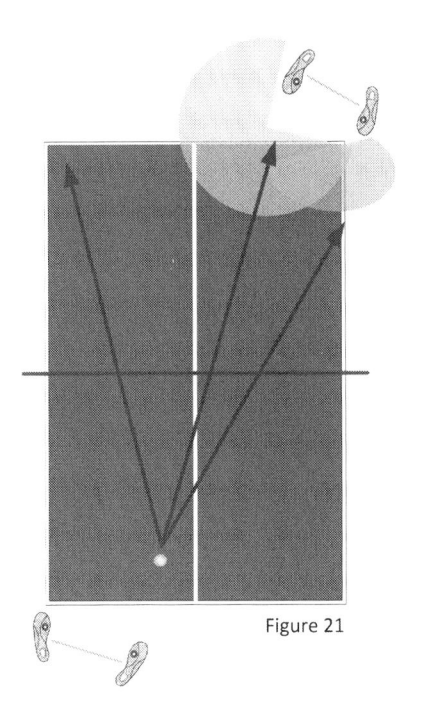

Figure 21

Figure 21 shows better options for shot selection as opposed to the player's choice in Figure 19. In this diagram, wide forehand (preferably with sidespin) will stretch the opponent's footwork. Wide backhand will lead to the tactics displayed in Figure 20, and a show to the middle is used to simply achieve a player's pin and to force the opponent to respond with a shot which will not have any threatening angles.

In Figure 21, the player has options for placement. First, is a shot slightly wider to the opponent's forehand which will force the opponent to move before attempting to execute the next stroke. Another alternative is to attack sharper to the backhand. Both of these placements allow player on the bottom of the diagram to maintain his position, while maximizing the movement of his adversary. Lastly, there is an option of producing a shot to the crossover point or point of indecision in an attempt to maintain an initiative and seek out other opportunities on subsequent shots.

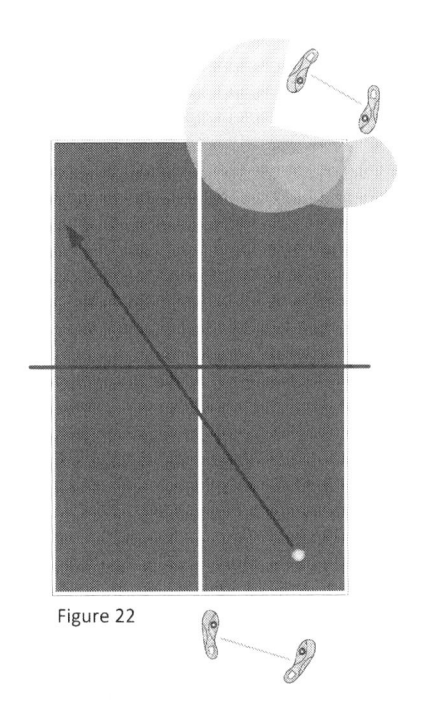

Figure 22

Figure 22 demonstrates a most conservative and yet very threatening option for a player's shot selection.

Finally, an alternative to the diagram displayed on Figure 19 is the diagram on Figure 22, which shows a very conservative and yet extremely dangerous option for the opponent. Simply placing the ball wide will create significant stress of the opponent's movement. If the shot carries even the slightest amount of sidespin in addition to the angle, it would create even more difficulties for the opponent. This tactic is risk averse and should be the first choice for player's in this position.

From the analysis of the positions described above, it is clearly visible that each player has to have a significant knowledge and understanding of these basic patterns. These patterns are extremely common on the court. Intelligent players purposefully drill these positions in order to learn to cope with these scenarios in the match. The concepts are simple – minimize your movement in order to maximize control. Maximize opponent's movement in order to minimize opponent's control. When the opportunity presents to take advantage of an easy return, only then will a smart player go for a winner. Until that moment, player's best option is to maneuver for advantage.

Tactical Dimensions

There are several facts that guide tactical decisions. These are similar to the one that explains the natural human movements and the differences in biomechanics for forehand and backhand execution and what kind of patterns fall out from these differences. However, there are others that should be well noted.

First, let's look again at the difference of the backhand and forehand movements. When playing lefties, a right handed player has to change his strategy and also tactics in order to properly create tactical opportunities. It is common for a left handed player to have a good and very stable backhand because they play a lot more right handed players whose ultimate shot is a cross court forehand. Right handed players frequently falter because they are unable to gain an advantage in their forehand cross court shots. This is because a backhand stroke is smaller than a forehand stroke. It takes a lot less time to block or counter the ball with the backhand rather than executing a lengthy forehand, which needs to involve much more body movement in its technique. Attempting to execute a fast shot too soon will allow the lefty to block the ball hard right back to the forehand to score the point. The tactical dimension involved here is time!

Where else does time come into the picture for a tactical combination? First and foremost a quick push to the body or wide and away from the player is one of the main tactics forcing the opponent to unreadily respond to a shot. Other examples are choppers who change the timing of their shot going from slow defense to quick counter attacks and vice versa and slow, spiny offensive player's opening shots that aim to get a slower higher block in return in order to set up a powerful kill. Sometimes, offensive players try to execute a timing tactic by chopping a fast ball away from the table in order to interfere with opponent's rhythm. It is extremely difficult to go from fast shot exchanges to slow ones. This type of tactic interferes with player's ability to do so. Finally, quick long serves is a tactic aimed to try to exploit the time constraints for a receiving player and hoping to get an easy, high ball in the middle of the table.

  Next tactical dimension is the spin variation. Offensive players can alter loops with flat shots as well as use deception in order to produce slow spiny and not so spiny shots with the same motion. Defensive players, especially players with anti or pips vary their approach to the ball so that the shot has different quantities of speed and spin. This tactic is heavily used for service and service returns.

  Height is yet another element. Some players have an extremely hard time with a high ball or sometimes just a slightly higher ball. Traditional penholders for the longest time had a weakness when they received a high ball to their backhand. Their grip was extremely limited to dealing with that ball because the arm and the wrist angle do not naturally bend in a way to return a high backhand ball with comfort. Frequently, penhold players would jump up in order to block that type of a shot. Surprisingly enough, there are also some players who struggle against a high quality lobbing game in the international arena, allowing players in desperate defense to regain the balance and seek out possible counter attacking opportunities.

Finally, there are tactics based on deception. These tactics are devised as a different type of a timing tactic. The aim of deceptive tactics is to lock the opponent in a position by forcing him to wait for the ball longer. This means that the player has to wait a little longer and read the ball quicker to get ready for an incoming shot. Deceptive strokes are extremely effective at any level.

When we put all of these dimensions together, we begin to realize that players do not ultimately pick out all of the tactics in their arsenal to play the match. How does the player know what tactic will work and which one will not? The tactics are selected based on the knowledge of the opponent and understanding of the opponent's game. The most effective way to win a match is by combining strategy with tactical combinations. Strategy outlines the general plan of attack and the tactics devise proper combinations of shots to satisfy strategic goals.

Considering many different tactical dimensions, for any given weakness, there are many different tactics available for player's disposal. The rest is left up to the execution of the tactic.

The Pin and a Switch

A successful tactic is set up using the very same principles of military history – suppression and maneuvering. In table tennis, however, it is best described as a pin and a switch. It was briefly described in the prior chapter, but let's look at the examples of pin and switch in further details.

A switch is a way to change the direction of the attacking shot. As noted by Michel Gadal, 80% of the shots come back to the general area where the shots have originated. This means that most of the players either do not have time and are not prepared to alter the placement, or decide to use attrition and defense in order to maintain their position after opponent's shot. Tactics, however, begin with an element of change. Therefore, when the player is able to attack one area of the table and then change the placement to attack another area, the player is switching the line of play.

There are many alternatives to switching the lines of play, but for the most part, the goal is to exhaust the opponent's ability to fend off the attack by constantly being able to vary the placement of the next shot in a sequence. A player capable of consistently and continuously switching the line of play will likely win the point because an opponent that is late for his shots will likely just aim to put the ball back on the table. With a focus to merely bringing the ball back on the table, his placement indeed will probably be in the same spot where the shots have originated from. Tactically, a smart opponent will have to try execute the so called "switch the switch" during the exchange in an attempt to regain the balance of the rally.

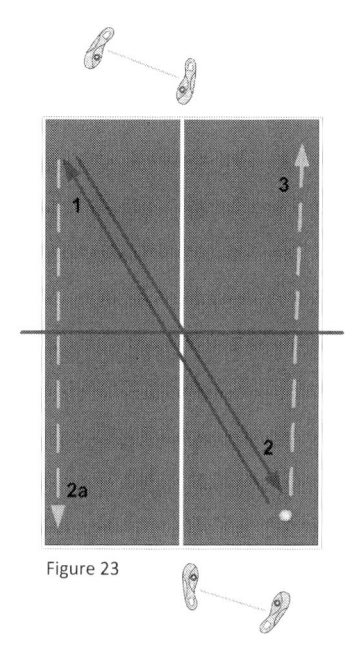

Figure 23

Figure 23 shows how after executing a shot identified by arrow 1, the player expects to receive a ball back in a spot displayed by arrow 2. The player's intention is to try to take advantage of the anticipated placement 2 and put the ball into opponent's backhand identified by a dashed arrow 3. The opponent, however, decides to take advantage of the player's position sooner switching the placement from predictable arrow 2, into dashed arrow 2a.

Consider a position in Figure 23. The player on the bottom of the diagram has just put the ball cross court and is preparing to attack his opponent down the line on the next shot. Meanwhile, the opponent decides to go down the line first in order to prevent his opponent from being able to produce a sharp angle to the backhand, but also to attack player's backhand side at the same time. Points during the rally can have as many switches as the players decide to execute. It depends largely in a player's ability to change the placement of his shots whenever a positional advantage or a threat from the opponent is recognized.

The best way to set up a switch, however, is with a pin. Imagine yourself drilling a forehand-backhand transition which is aimed to improving movements of forehand and backhand execution in succession. Most of the time, this type of a drill can be done successfully with a consistent pace. Yet, if you change the timing of the shots during this drill, all of a sudden, it will be extremely hard to maintain the exchange.

This example shows that players are generally more fluid during evenly timed rhythmic intervals, but respond erratically as the timing demands alter. Try to rush the forehand for a quick shot and then return to return a slower backhand shot and vice versa. It will be extremely difficult.

Humans overall tend to react a lot better to a constant sustained rhythm, rather than a constantly changing one. That is noted in everything from music, dance, and obviously sports. It is also a whole of a lot easier to accelerate in the speed of the movement rather than slow movement down. The reason for it is that healthy human hearts are designed to respond quicker to increasing and sustaining body's physical load. Slowing down of the heart rate after higher intensity activity takes a lot more time. This is where the pin becomes an invaluable tactical tool. It establishes a certain predictable rhythm which can then be challenged.

When the opponent is pinned, his responses are aimed at merely controlling the return. The pin is accomplished with strong, quick, threatening shots which do not leave any time for the opponent to move in order to counter the attack. Therefore, a pinned player usually mounts his defense and plants himself in a fixed position ready for defense. The issue with this position is that the pinned player halts all of the movement and if you observe your own game with an unbiased, independent point of view, you will realize that it is a lot harder to attain movement from a dead stop, rather than continue moving throughout the stroke execution with minimal motions. The cause of this "anomaly" is balance.

Human biomechanics heavily rely on transfer of weight in order to attain movement. When we walk, our arms naturally swing in order to achieve balance transfer. This is especially visible in the way we run. Therefore, when the player halts movement for defense, his movement is limited to small distances. In terms of strokes, the player is unable use his whole body from a static position. He will be limited to executing short, quick off the bounce strokes by using incoming pace and spin of the ball, which means that a wide, deep movement will be harder to achieve. This is exactly what the switch after a pin accomplishes. The pin locks the player from being able to quickly move, and then the switch is used to challenge the player's footwork.

This explains the types of the shots used to win points and games in lower and intermediate levels of table tennis. A simple attacking shot directly into the player, followed by an even a slightly redirected next shot usually wins the point. In the higher level though, this is not enough. The defense of the players is a lot stronger and the players are very well prepared to defend in a proper way – placing the defensive shots into the zones of the attacking player where the attacker is unable to produce a strong shot.

What are these zones? The answer to this question explains a proper way to unpin yourself whenever the opponent's offense has you pressed against the ropes.

When a player is attacked directly into the backhand in a close to the table position, there is not enough time to loop the ball back. The first opening shot is usually strong enough to commence an attack but is not aimed to be a point winner. Looping requires a larger stroke which takes time. It takes time that the player typically will not have due to the close distance to the table. The usual response to defend this shot is a block or a counter, but the block is usually followed with another offensive shot, which will be stronger than the opening one. This is the moment when the player becomes pinned. If the opponent continues to block the ball directly to the same spot or just slightly move it, he will need to rely on attrition to win the point, which at the higher level is a lot less likely. Instead, it is best to attempt to unpin yourself in an attempt to create an opportunity for a counter attack.

Removal of the pin is demonstrated in Figure 24. The player at the bottom of the diagram is pinned by his opponent. There are several spots where this player can place the ball in order to effectively unpin himself. Wide forehand and backhand zones are valid options, however, considering all players' training, most players, especially at the highest levels can follow up with strong shots from those zones even when those players are on a move.

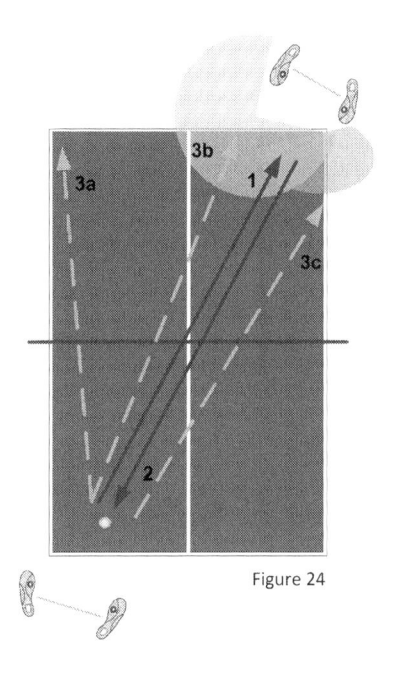

Figure 24

Figure 24 demonstrates options available to the player when attempting to unpin from numerous exchanges marked by arrow 1 and 2. Wide forehand and wide backhand zones marked by 3a and 3c are logically obvious, but players always train footwork in order to effectively cover those zones. The middle, however, is a better option because it forces the opponent to decide whether to move a step to the forehand or a step to the backhand.

The best alternative in this position is to target the opponent's middle. If the ball is successfully placed in this zone, the opponent will be unable to sustain the attack with the same force. The opponent also will be unable to initiate a strong attack by switching a line of play from those positions because his angles from the middle of the table are not sharp enough to create a significant amount of pressure.

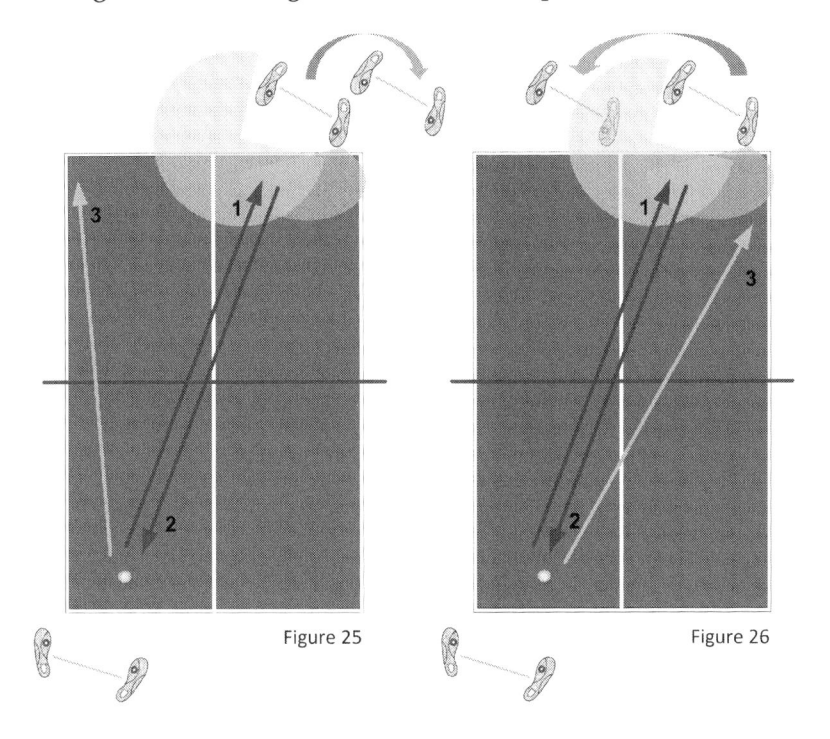

Figure 25

Figure 26

Figure 25 the opponent at the top of the diagram is responding to the player's shot down the middle as a way to unpin himself. The player takes a step to the backhand in order to use a forehand on a shot to the middle. Yet, by doing so, he opens up wide forehand for attack.

Figure 26 Similarly to the Figure 25, the player at the top of the diagram attempts to respond to a shot into the middle with a backhand by taking a small step to the middle of the table. However, this would allow the player at the bottom of the diagram to attack wide backhand.

Since a switch from the middle does not produce a significant advantage with the angles available, the only option left is again to try to pin the player with a follow up attack to the backhand. Yet, in order to return the ball from the crossover point, the opponent has to take a small step to the middle of the table to use the backhand or step farther away from the table to use a forehand. If the player moves to use a forehand, he opens up a forehand as demonstrated in the following diagrams on Figure 25. Meanwhile, if the opponent moves to the middle of the table to use the backhand on the shot to the elbow, as displayed in Figure 26, he opens up a wide backhand area for attack.

Thus, the opponent with an early initiative was eventually forced to give up his initiative using a few well-placed controllable shots. This is one more example proving that placement is a lot more important than strength of a shot.

Since we have just covered how a player can successfully unpin himself, is there a way to resist to the opponent's attempt unpin himself? How can someone counteract the opponent in this scenario?

This is done similarly to the switching of the switch principle, where a change in direction by one player can be changed again by his opponent in order to keep the opponent from gaining an absolute advantage. Unpinning involves using the point of indecision to hamper the player's movement. Figure 27 demonstrates how an attacking player can target his opponent's point of indecision right back in order to retain the initiative and prevent an opponent from successfully freeing himself from a pin.

Figure 27

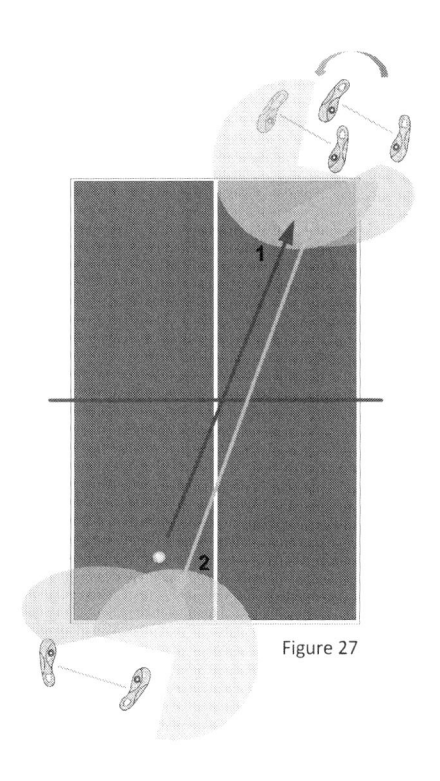

Figure 27 demonstrates how a player at the top of the diagram can prevent a player at the bottom from unpinning himself. This is done by returning the shot aimed to the middle (arrow 1) back to the opponent's middle (arrow 2). This placement limits the opponent's ability to sustain a strong attack.

A position where both players can counteract each other's threats then turns into an encounter resembling a match between two sumo wrestlers. Both are strong enough to resist each other, however the winner of the point will be the player able to continually place the ball into a proper zone and the one who is quick enough to create an opportunity for a strong attack with his movement by using Wayne Gretzky's principle of not moving after a puck, but rather, moving to a position where the puck will be. Thus, anticipation and positional understanding is highly important for this type of a rally.

Take a look at most of the table tennis rallies on the professional level and they would surely indicate exactly the following patterns to constantly play out on the court. These are the methods that can challenge even the best players. Hence, there is no need to force a monster shot early. Small positional gains will eventually lead to opportunities of being capitalized into points.

Development of Tactics

How does one learn to master tactics? Certainly, many combinations and tactical patterns can be created, but what is the most important element in learning tactics? How does one get better in tactical application?

The knowledge of tactical positions is of course immensely important, yet there is another skill that is synonymous with tactical development. This has already been mentioned in prior chapters. It is placement control. If one is unable to control placement, then tactical combinations cannot be applied to their best extent. A slight mistake in placement of a ball to the player's elbow sends the ball right into the opponent's forehand. Do it a few times, and you find yourself trailing a few points. Try to produce a wide ball and miss by only an inch a few times and you're in a deficit that will be close to impossible to recover.

Placement control is of outmost importance. Obviously understanding of the opponent's positional advantages and positional advantages of your own is necessary for proper shot selection. This, however, will take experience and knowledge of "thyself." Every player need to know their own comfort zones, the positions where they feel comfortable to sustain the attack, and the angles they can comfortably use in those positions.

In chess, tactics are learned from books. There are special purpose tactical books which outlines different tactical goals that will be achieved and draw out numerous types of positions. A chess player has to evaluate a given position in the book and find a winning tactical combination, whether it is to win a pawn, a piece, a rook, a queen, or to achieve a checkmate. The same can be accomplished in table tennis. While there are no books that provide a large list of player's tactical exercises, a player can create his own, even the most basic diagrams to help explain positions, movements, and frequently occurring scenarios of the table.

If the player drafts out a model of the table on a simple piece of paper and simply looks for a video of one of his favorite players, he can draw numerous exchanges of various shots executed in the video in arrows similarly to diagrams in this section of the book. Now, imagine which shot would have been best in a given point. Do you see some potential opportunities? Is there a placement which would be better in a given shot sequence? Why was the player not able to place the ball in that direction? Was the player too far, too slow, or in an awkward position? Or was he attempting to score a winner too early? This is the type of analysis of table tennis positions that will be helpful to learn and understand tactics to a much deeper level. Skill wise, tactical training can also be improved with drills.

Tactical skills are developed by configuring special purpose drills that continuously aim to apply specific shot combinations. Each shot is aimed to improve a tactical element. Drills can be set up to achieve accurate placement as well as to set up a scenario that calls for dynamic placement change. In addition to placement, drills can be instrumented to changing elements of the speed, spin, and height during exchange. In training, the drills should aim to setup the player's strongest shots. In the match, however, tactics should be picked to work opponent's weaknesses.

The best tactical players are usually the most experienced and disciplined ones. They are prepared to patiently rally for an advantage and are keen to recognize the right opportunities to go for a win. That is why it takes such a long time to get better in this game. At some point, the player has to learn to apply strategies and tactics in a match in order to become a better player simply for a fact that at a high level there is an antidote to every player's sting and it takes more than one blow to score a point.

The Mental Game

"The greatest discovery of my generation is that a human being can alter his life by altering his attitudes."

- William James

Many books on mental game recently emerged on the market. They all offer great insights over a wide range of theories and methods that can be utilized to optimize player's performance during competition. The methods vary, but for the most part, they teach to maintain focus, concentration, and the magical "zone" which allows the player to peak their heightened state of awareness, assertiveness, and responsiveness.

Some books suggest concentration routines, others self-motivation and self-reinforcement. A few emphasize analysis of the momentum of the match and teach how to control the momentum by providing various ways to seek out and to create opportunities that affect opponent's mental state while retaining self-control. However, all these approaches have minor flaw in common – they all provide generic solutions that are supposed to suit the masses. In reality, there are no remedies of the mental game that are ideal for everyone. Each individual requires his own personalized look into mental performance. This is simply because every player has a different strength and weakness in the mental game and therefore requires an individual mental training routine.

Professional athletes, especially the ones who are well compensated by their organizations mandate a frequency of professional mental training. They hire sports psychiatrists and subject the players under a rigorous mental training regimen which is tailored independently for each athlete. The better prepared players produce better results and the organizations are careful to get a full return on their investment. However, this book is for general audience and the general audience has a significant void in information available to players regarding mental game preparation, especially from a strategic player development perspective. My goal is to continue filling in the missing gaps of information and this section is intended to provide the initial amount of material necessary for a serious player.

This part of the book is not about a proposed new mental method. Many people that know me as a player are well aware of my own mental game struggles and shortcomings that I have been working to improve. I am far from an expert to suggest a new methodology, yet my flaws caused me to leap into a world of knowledge towards gaining a better understanding of my personal mental characteristics and the many elements of the mental game that "make me tick."

I recognized my struggles early and the first step I have made toward improving my mental game began by exploring a vast amount of mental game topics. I made a decisive effort to discover the very psychological factors that have impeded my abilities to reach the goals well within my reach - goals that I undoubtedly was capable of attaining given my focus and intensity of the training. Oddly, most of the mental weaknesses in my game did not generate from table tennis skills or athletic abilities. They originated in other parts of my life and the many experiences I encountered along the way. I discovered secrets of my own behavior and these discoveries gave me hints on what I needed to work on in order to perform better under pressure.

This chapter is devoted to the discoveries that helped me understand the needs of my mental game since they will undoubtedly apply to many other players aiming to achieve higher levels of the game. Again, I am by no means an expert, but I have gained a very deep level of understanding of what it takes for a player to walk the "high road." I realize now after my quest, that a mental game is the key element that impedes most players' ability to realize their full potential. A player capable of finding a way to open and maintain access the full arsenal of their strengths is the one who is best positioned for ongoing improvement and success.

With these thoughts, let's proceed further to learn how we function, how we think, and how we can use this knowledge to unleash our play.

Mental Basics

Most people bring up the mental game when observing or experiencing a moment of extreme climax in the game - a tight match with an end within a match point. It becomes synonymous with pressure, nervousness, choking – all are negative associations that make the word "mental" even more troublesome. However, there are many different types of a mental game and not all of the elements pertain to the crucial moments. Certainly, player's performance in a close match and the outcome will be influenced more by the most mentally prepared player, however what does it truly mean to be mentally prepared and how can one allow himself to play in comfort?

If you survey the players around your club and ask them on their preferences to playing the matches, you will find that some players perform better when they are ahead in points, while others achieve their best performance when they are playing behind. It is only natural that some desire different positions for their ultimate performance. Similarly, some players have better ability to close out the match on a first chance, while others need a little buffer in order to emerge victorious. These are the mental comfort zones.

These comfort zones are fundamental principles of "knowing thyself" and they underline the basic mental strategies. When a player knows his own game and is aware of his own mental attitudes and preferences in his matches, the player should make sure to play within his preferences and set the tone of the game in a way to facilitate the best performance. Thus, player's strategy in a match should not only focus on playing the strokes, but must also take the mental preferences into consideration.

If a player is aware that his best mental state in a match exists when he is able to secure an early lead and then dictate the tempo of the match by being the first to take the game within a game point, then it is important to concentrate on creating this type of a winning environment. This player needs to start strong right away and aim to maintain his lead throughout.

Another player might have a different preference. Let's say another player likes to trail back a few points only to close in on the lead in the end of the game. His peak in concentration occurs when he finally closes the gap. He plays a lot more comfortably in a pressure of a deuce point because of his level of excitement, and therefore his source of focus originates from the challenge of being down and still emerging victorious. This player's plan is to maintain a position on the heels of his adversary until he can close in on point deficit at the end of the match and utilize his superior attitude under pressure.

What would happen if both of these players play a match? As long as the first player maintains his solid lead, he will be victorious, however, the larger will be the point difference or the closer the game will lead to the end, the more comfortable the second player will be in attempting to catch up to his favorable deuce position. In this situation, both of the players complement each other's mental games.

Their mental games are ideally suited to challenge each other's mental strategies. With all skills being equal, the match result between these players will depend on which player is able to fully realize the mental strategy and the one who will make less unforced errors in the process.

It is obvious in this scenario that the first player will win the match as long as he is able to maintain the lead. However, if the first player is not as aggressive and does not secure an early lead, what would be the mental comfort zone of the second player? Will the second player assume a dominating position and take this match to the end, or will his attention and concentration fade away due to his mental preference of playing from behind? What would further happen if the second player will be the first to reach the deuce? His heightened level of arousal might be negated by the very fact that there was less challenge without a need to recover the point deficit. Can this player play his best game when he is not pushed on a brink of his ultimate level of concentration? Would he be capable of closing out the game? The match?

This is the moment when many players begin to struggle particularly because they do not realize how difficult it truly is to close out the match. As the point lead get smaller, the pressure gets tougher. Many players in advantageous positions begin to take unnecessary chances in an attempt to rush a kill shot in a tactic or to serve an ace. Every easy shot missed seems to set the tone for yet another mistake. This is the point when most players begin to deviate from their strategy and frequently start using tactics that are playing into the opponent's strengths. There are even players that get so nervous at that vital moment that they begin to play by chance by serving long to the opponent, hoping the opponent will be the one to make an easy mistake instead of ultimately playing their own game to score the point. This is a very poor play from a statistical and mental standpoint, but occurs often enough to be mentioned.

  For some players attempting to close the match, it feels like walking the quicksand. The more they try to get out of the sand and scoring the point, the deeper they sink by giving up more points in the process.

  The outcome of the match will depend on the player's ability to concentrate on the task at hand. Hence, every player needs to know and understand how to maintain and raise the level of concentration during critical points in the match.

  These are the very basic mental game fundamentals. The players are subjected to all kind of conditions that occur in the match with different type of efforts necessary to achieve victory. Instead of constantly learning through experience by trial and error, let's review many topics of the mental game that every player needs to understand in order to find better solutions quicker – with fewer trials and less errors.

Attitude

William James, the first educator of psychology in the United States, famously commented that "the first lecture on psychology I ever heard was the first I ever gave." Strangely enough, I began to recognize the same feelings regarding my own experience reading and learning more about sports psychology and now documenting the thoughts that collectively settled in my mind.

The side effect of having to search for the truth inside of many mental game "secrets" and especially sharing my findings with other players and coaches has opened up my view on the mental game to a deeper paradigm – it began to alter my attitude towards the mental game. It no longer has a strong mystical and especially negative association, but rather transformed the meaning of the word into a definition of a challenge. After all, isn't challenge is what every player seeks in this game? William James identified this paradigm with another quote "The greatest discovery of my generation is that a human being can alter his life by altering his attitudes."

What does it mean to alter the attitude and how does that fit into the mental part of the game, you might ask. A player who "chokes" or struggles with a match does not seem to have a problem with attitude but rather a problem initiating a proper action or overdoing it. His attitude is to win, but the result does not always align with the attitude.

The attitude I am talking about here is not an attitude within the last point, but rather a long term strategic attitude toward a refinement and development of a proper mental game – essentially continuous learning.

My coach, Gerald Reid, said a perfect phrase for an ultimate highpoint of the match after yet another close, but losing match. "You worked extremely hard to get to the moment to close out the match, why would you get too careless or too careful now? You worked too hard to let it go its own course." This is a very factual statement of the mental state of too many players during the critical moment of the game. We all seem to work hard on our physical skills, but we do not prepare our mental skills for the moment when we will eventually improve and arrive in a dominant, critical position against our adversaries, especially when those adversaries are higher skilled, highly regarded players.

Strategic development of the player must always take mental game into consideration. This means building up a player's mental game in unison with the physical skills so that the player can learn to play his shots, following appropriate strategy and tactics, with focus and concentration in any point, whether it is a first point of the game or the last. Instead, however, we frequently find players whose body language shows extreme signs of distress. Players scream at themselves with anger, insulting themselves with a wild array of curses, kick, stomp, and throw their paddles. While few scarce players really need this type of motivation and strive under such conditions, most will find that it is a symptom of poor mental game, or an ugly mental tactic aimed to distract the opponent, rather than a methodology for heightening ones' senses.

How should the player train his mental strengths? First and foremost, it is done with a deliberate effort for the player to try to understand him or herself. The player needs to open up his senses during various matches and note what allows him or her to play with ease and what seems to create inner struggles.

Using the previous chapter's example of two opponents with different mental preferences, it is easy to note a direct relationship over the type of the game that opponent imposes and the player's attitude toward the match. Some opponents seem to impose a very uncomfortable type of a game for the player by producing a vast variety of undesired shots - too slow, too easy, too weird, too strong, too awkward, too soft. These feelings are the very hints that allow the player to understand their mental needs and mental distractions.

For example, a common way some players break the rhythm of their opponents is with their purposeful image of being disinterested in the match. A few wild shots made here and there, a scream of disappointment, a sign of mental distress – walking head down, voicing complaints out loud by blaming the light, paddle, equipment, floor, shoes, etc. Acting as if the individual just does not care whether he wins or loses, makes the shot or misses. The methods of such image delivery are endless, but ultimately this type of action subconsciously has a strong impact on a player. If only for a few seconds a player begins to analyze the opponent and his behavior, that player will be suckered into distraction mode leading to a much more challenging task of trying to win the match.

The only way to protect against this type of interruption is by knowing what kind of opponent action has a significant impact on player's performance. A prepared player knows this information upfront and already has routines worked out to negate all kinds of strategic or tactical mental threats. Against a slow opponent, a well prepared player is ready for patient, long, and grueling game. Against a fast opponent, the player is ready for quick movements. Against a "weird" opponent, the player is ready with a proper strategy. Against an opponent with mental tactics, the player is ready to ignore the opponent and is focused on maintaining his concentration. These few examples of preparedness out of many clear the useless "noise" in a match, opening up room for a nice clear line of thought, and a smooth, clean game.

Let's change the attitude for a minute and try to get mentally prepared for a match. Think of a moment when you felt that you had the match clinched in your hands only to find it slip away. What is the first thought that comes to mind when you visualize that moment. Did you feel upset? Do you blame the environment around you? Did this scenario occur at least a few times consistently with the same outcome? Do you even know what happened? Can you identify the mistake? What was the first mistake? Did more mistakes follow? Perhaps you feel that the opponent has gotten lucky. Was it just not your day?

The answers to these questions begin to expose all the very "holes" that exist in your mental game. Instead of dwelling on the outcome which cannot be changed, let's try to change the attitude by finding a solution to the very problems that occurred within the match. It all starts with asking yourself some tough questions, which some players avoid altogether and attempt to erase prior matches from their memory. The right way, however, it to face the truth head on. These questions must be asked and as often as one can. The answers will provide hints on how a player can learn to deal with the given troublesome scenario.

For every question you can ask yourself – continue further. Ask more questions and keep on asking until you find a solution over what exactly would have changed the outcome of the match. Then, create a contract in a booklet for yourself to follow that will guide you if you find yourself in a similar position from the moment forward. This document will now serve as your personal play book.[18]

For a given play, your answers are recorded and remembered! No more guessing or coming up with solutions on the spot by "trying things out." Trying means

---

[18] Serious training in many disciplines is divided into theoretical and practical. For some reason table tennis is almost always taught on the table, working out with the ball, while in essence the physics involved in ball flight, and stroke execution along with the mental preparation really require a much more sophisticated learning methodology. There are certainly topics that should ideally be taught in table tennis classroom instead of the court. I believe we should not shy away from traditional classroom training. For example, firemen consistently attend training in class and on the training grounds. In chess, there is no substitute to classroom time allocated for game analysis. In military, flying a plane, driving a tank, or shooting a cannon involves teaching many elements involved in operation of the weapon and use of geographical characteristics of the area where the weapon is planned to be utilized on the map, rather than in the field.

uncertainty, but having a predetermined response means planning. Well established plans have a proven track record of producing better results over time.

    Remember the old joke "How many psychiatrists does it take to change a light bulb? One, but the light bulb needs to want to change!" Changing the attitude means taking the mental aspects of the game seriously, without making it sound like it's OK to keep testing the waters. It's almost like playing a known opponent over and over using different strategy while opponent's weaknesses are clearly known and understood. Unless you're purposefully trying to play this opponent differently to learn a new skill, there does not need to be a trial period to come up with a proper plan for winning the match. Why change the winning game? Same goes for why continue playing a losing one?

    Over time, this contract or the booklet with predetermined responses will begin to outline player's experience. The faster this information is documented, the sooner the experience can be reapplied with greater chances for success because realistically speaking, unless we purposefully train our minds to remember loads of information, we will eventually forget the successful solutions we came up with some time ago for a given match scenario. This will again lead us to experimentation and likely to result in a few needlessly lost opportunities. On the other hand, keeping up with the constant and relentless analysis will only lead to better preparedness for a match.

    As if studying for a big exam, the player can open the material and review it before the tournament especially if the draws are made up prior to the tournament and the opponents are known beforehand. No more simple brainless play of coached instructions because a coach is there to hold the player's hand with valuable advice at the right time. Instead, the player can take responsibility into his own hands and collaborate with the coach through his own preparedness.

This is a complete change of the attitude, from reactionary into strategic, focused, and forward thinking.

Concentration

There is a teen comedy called "Accepted" where a high school student's college applications get rejected and he decides to create his own college by faking the documents and creating this new imaginary college's web site. As soon as the web pages for the new fake college are created, other students with similar rejection letters begin to apply, receiving automatic acceptance to attend the new school. One of the funny characters in this movie who signs up to attend a newly formed college decides that as part of the class curriculum he would like to learn how to blow things up with his mind. His goal is to master concentration in a way that would allow him to unleash this hidden power of explosion. Every time he tries to concentrate, his already funny looking face cringes with a hilarious expression. This is certainly comical in a movie. But, does concentration really require this much effort? As a matter of fact, can a person really concentrate quickly and on demand?

Concentration is a state of heightened senses and alertness, but the way our human minds work, it is extremely difficult to enter this state on demand. Writers, for example, utilize slow, smooth and gentle music to relax to settle their thoughts so they could write. Athletes, especially in various contact sports for the longest time turned to angry fighting music to enter the state of preparedness for the upcoming clash. Athletes involved in precision sports develop pre and post-shot routines that allow the players to repeatedly enter a comfortable state of concentration for an upcoming execution of a skill. They also utilize imagery techniques for mental preparation of an upcoming task execution.

Each type of a sport has its own appropriate method to achieve focus necessary for the best performance. The method that works for one sport, will not always work for the other. Antagonistic sports, like table tennis, where players play each other, need a different approach to achieve concentration rather than precision sports such as shooting or golf. In their book "Winning Table Tennis," Dan Seemiller and Mark Holowchak mention that while imagery techniques can be applied for both sports, they have limited application of imagery techniques in table tennis: "Imagery is more effective for closed skills than open skills. Closed skills are simple mechanical skills over which you have much control. An example is the golf swing or the table tennis serve. Open skills are more complex, and external factors come to bear more significantly. For example, a table tennis rally."

Thus, precision sports allow the athletes more time to focus because players control all aspects of the mechanical execution. They wait until they are ready and they control all the movements of a given technique without external factors, while in table tennis, there is a lot less time to prepare shot to shot as the ball can be sent in many directions with different speed and spin. In precision sports, the execution of the skill always starts from the beginning of the skill and ends upon the execution of it. In table tennis, the point does not end until either of the players misses a shot. Hence, each of the shots and their respective set of technical skills in a table tennis rally require concentration – from the start of the point, all the way to the end.

If a human being is unable to quickly enter the state of concentration, what does it mean to concentrate and achieve focus? How does one know that a state of concentration has been successfully achieved?

The answers to these questions demand a deeper insight into human behavior. Cognitive psychology which studies how human beings think, perceive, and learn explains that there are several types of thoughts that occur within our minds. Some thoughts require purposeful thinking, while others seem to produce results without any purposeful actions. Think about it, when we walk, talk, eat, run, etc., we do not tell ourselves purposeful instructions for any of the following activities. All the actions involved in accomplishing these activities seem to happen automatically. This automatic ability to do something is referred to as an action accomplished by a subconscious mind. The conscious mind, on the other hand, is something that requires us to purposefully process a certain action.

Conscious mind is engaged most commonly during activities where our mind does not have an immediate way to access information about these events from prior examples. One of such main activities is learning, when we attempt to accomplish something new that we have not done in the past. Recall yourself learning to skate, bike ride, or swim and you will probably remember that you had to engage your mind to control the movements necessary for the task. At first, there was a feeling of awkwardness as you learned how to maintain balance, learn how to breathe, and learn proper movement. Then, after a few times of continuing the same thing, you were able to shelf those feeling and could replicate the movements without purposeful thoughts. This smooth transition occurs when the knowledge of the activity begins to transition from a conscious to the subconscious mind. At that moment, a very interesting thing happens. The heightened level of concentration is no longer necessary to accomplish a desired task!

Thus, concentration and focus is really only necessary when an individual is trying to accomplish a given task without sufficient prior knowledge and experience. If a given task has been repeated numerous times with success, our minds are capable to taking control of our body movements to repeat the same actions. Some people call it muscle memory, but in reality muscles do not have memory. These are actions from the library of activities that our brains can accomplish without purposeful engagement of our conscious mind.

If we do not need to concentrate or focus when we have achieved a sufficient prior repetition of a given task, then why do we need to concentrate and how can we explain that a phenomenon where a player still misses an easy shot, especially when he must have executed thousands if not millions of the same shots during training throughout the years?

To explain the reasons for this uncanny scenario, let's first look at the player's training. Most players are capable of achieving a high level of repetition of an extremely high quality shot in a training environment. The training environment is well known to the player and the exercises over time become familiar and extremely comfortable. The placement of the next ball in a sequence is mostly predetermined and well controlled. The player's subconscious mind quickly finds the automatic responses to a given shot and requires no purposeful effort from the conscious mind. Therefore, training based on repetition, especially with identical placement is a relatively simple skill that can be developed in a short amount of time. However, if within a given exercise an occasional ball is placed away from the intended return zone, most players, will not even respond to the changed placement and simply look at the ball. The reason is that the subconscious mind controls the player's movements as if on autopilot. The "autopilot" is configured to only respond to a ball in a given area on the table.

  A ball placed into another zone requires the player to disengage the "autopilot" in order to deviate from preprogrammed automatic movements. This requires turning on the conscious mind and allowing the brain to control the body. The problem is that conscious thoughts engage human senses. Now, perception of the ball's movement, its speed, spin, trajectory, and the feeling of the current body position along with analyzing the shot for best shot selection automatically cause a delay in the responses. This is merely a scenario that occurs within the training exercise if the ball is placed into a player's unexpected zone. The match has a lot more challenges as the opponent always tries to make things difficult for the player by constantly changing the placement of the ball, its spin, speed, trajectory, and height.

With so many elements of the game constantly changing, it is extremely tough for subconscious mind to come up with proper responses, especially in the beginning of the match. Playing a familiar or clearly weaker opponent is the only time when it becomes easier to achieve smooth play right from the start. Generally, though, only by the end of the match the players collect adequate information on the opponent's placement choices and shot selection to approach shots with better results. The problem, though, is that the game is too short. The players simply cannot afford waiting for their subconscious mind to engage in order to improve the quality of their play. If they wait, they will face an extremely daunting task of having to catch up, which is much harder to do and therefore will be less likely to succeed. Consequently, much of the struggling game plays out with a set of thoughts controlled by a conscious mind.

Human being's conscious mind is very different from its subconscious counterpart. Subconscious mind is able to execute multiple tasks at once. Imagine walking. There are many things that the mind figures out how to do. The mind automatically figures out how to walk, how big steps to make, how to keep balance, how to avoid obstacles like puddles or rocks all at the same time. Now think about something recent, whether is a chore that needs to be done, school, work, or anything else. Can you try to think about two separate things at the same time like a chore and what you will have for dinner or schoolwork and a new movie that you would like to go see? Conscious mind cannot handle multiple thoughts. It requires deliberate focus on a single thought at a time. A person can certainly switch his focus from one thought to another, but the first thought has to complete prior to a new thought being able to be processed. This is the reason why achieving heightened level of concentration requires a special approach.

During the match, there are many thoughts that go through the mind of players. Players take their time to preplan their strategy, analyze the opponent, and devise tactics. These are necessary thoughts in between points. Then, there are additional thoughts that also venture into player's minds. "I missed that shot", "I made that shot", "I need to tweak my execution in such a way", "I cannot believe I've missed it", "I know I will make it", etc. These thoughts, also called selftalk, are either factual which describe what has occurred, analytical which determine what went wrong, projective which try to predict the future outcome, or simply behavioral which merely expressing the inner feelings.

Some thoughts can provide valuable information in order to make an adjustment to the player's game. Yet, other thoughts are generally nothing but distractions. The conscious mind, however, does not focus on identifying the thoughts into specific types, but rather simply continues the thought pattern until a new thought comes up along the way.

Thus, the player whose conscious mind is in a state of processing one thought will be unable to perform another task until the conscious mind begins to process the thoughts pertaining to a new task. Imagine a player getting ready to return opponent's serve. This player needs to be ready to return the ball, but he is not ready to respond with actions quickly if his mind is presently busy processing other thoughts. Initiating a proper action becomes even more difficult if the current thoughts going through the head of the player are full of fears of making a mistake.

The best state of concentration is when the mind is clear of thoughts. Then, the player is capable of engaging the conscious mind to quickly handle a new task as well as enabling the subconscious mind to automatically produce responses to known, familiar tasks. However, how do you achieve a clear mind? Seems that anytime you try not to think about anything, the mind says "I am trying not to think about anything"! This is exactly why players cannot force themselves into a state of concentration by telling themselves that they need to concentrate.

The most effective methods to clear the mind and achieve focus are through breathing exercises and learning how to zero in all of the attention on the ball. The method of attaining concentration works by eliminating mind's "heavy" useless thoughts by replacing them with very simple and basic thoughts for the player to process. These thoughts vanish quickly upon the need to execute a new task.

A player conducting breathing exercises naturally begins to focus in the actual way the breathing is accomplished by the body, which blocks out all other thoughts. Watching the ball for example, does the same thing but replaces other thoughts with only remaining thought of simple descriptive nature about the ball. "The ball is in front of me." "I am watching the ball." Whichever method a player prefers to adopt into his game, both methods work extremely well to enable the player' state of readiness. However, there is yet another method available to the player.

Because the conscious mind only allows a single thought to be handled at a time, if a player is thinking strategic or tactical thoughts, like "I need to place the ball to the forehand", the player will also achieve a very good level of concentration by preplanning a response.

After finding a concentration method that works best for the player and adopting it as the basis of the readiness aspect of the mental game, the player will be a lot more prepared for the match with better outcomes. This is especially true if the method becomes a vital part of every point preparation routine – whether the service or the receive, whether the opening, or the following exchange.

As you can see, concentration is achieved naturally, not forcefully. The reason why concentration cannot be attained on demand is because it takes a bit of time to clear the mind of useless thoughts that will impede the execution of the following task. However, this is just a beginning, because the hardest part is not reaching concentration, but maintaining one throughout the match. The concentration levels will peak and fade, but if the method of concentration is repeated point-to-point, the concentration level will be maintained.

There are however, times when the players cannot seem to lift the burden of their thoughts even with their best efforts to execute a predetermined concentration routine. Let's proceed to the next chapter to understand human behavior in the face of a possible failure.

Failure

You see this frequently at many tournaments. Promising players, sometimes even very strong players begin to play nervously. At times, they do not even resemble themselves in the way they play the game. They look slow, uncomfortable and get extremely upset. All of a sudden a promising champion is simply – afraid to lose!

As with any antagonistic sports where players play each other, the match will eventually end with one player emerging a winner and another a loser. Obviously no player wants to be referred to as a loser, even when the loss is well substantiated, but not all players will be winners either.

Table tennis is different from other sports where there are possibilities of being undefeated, like boxing where there is an extra bonus for never suffering defeat. In table tennis, at one time or another, everyone loses. Looking at the top 20 players in the world their statistics show that they always go through loses especially when facing similarly skilled opponents within the same top 20 ranks. Even the number one player in the world does not remain undefeated for a prolonged amount of time. If it is a natural occurrence in our game, why are some players scared of losing? Why do they lose their senses, and get angry with themselves, especially when it is common knowledge that fears of losing will indeed harm the player's game even more?

Improvement in table tennis seems to carry an unofficial responsibility. The higher level of the game an improving player achieves, the higher is the level of recognition and almost a sociological status the player assumes. This is all obviously fake because there are no official statuses other than world, or country ranks. Yet most of the players push themselves too hard to make the list of top X number of players that when they get close to their goals or begin to slide off their spot, their mental game totally shuts down.

Unfortunately it gets even worse. Players also pick up pressure from external sources – coaches, organizations, and for junior players – parents. Everyone seems to want to prove that their player is a star, but isn't it just too much pressure to bear? Players forced under the stress of producing results will falter more often than not. Such players open the door to their emotions, which in turn bring about nervousness. Nervousness brings lack of assertiveness and response. Down the road, for most, this brings a loss.

I recall watching a tournament where both players in a final of an intermediate section were so nervous that both kept missing easy shots and were bumping the ball back and forth as if they just picked up the paddle for the first time.

This behavior is not uncommon. The question is how do you prevent it? How does the player prepare himself to play his game without preset handicaps? In order to answer this question, we need to back track a little bit and try to find a purpose of playing the game.

Most players who play this sport did not immerse themselves into the action by attempting to become world champions right from the start. Maybe as a farsighted dream, yes, we all need dreams, but in reality, if we count how many players dream to attain the desired title, how many actually achieve it? The chances are miniscule. Lots of kids in the US want to be the President of the United States of America and while it looks extremely cute for the parents to see their child utter the words, only select few will get that chance and only because these select few will someday hatch plans to follow through on their dreams and manage to get lucky with recognizing opportunities that may present themselves along the way.

Even if a young player enters a sophisticated training program, his future results are not guaranteed to take him to the number one spot in the world. The aims are very modest. The ultimate goal is to discover the inner potential of a given individual. As the training progresses from the initial beginning stages to the advanced stages, a lot more is learned about the player's abilities, speed of learning new material, flexibility, creativity, and any other factors that ultimately influence the next steps of the training regiments. The only thing that is guaranteed is that the player will be subjected to an immense amount of training and will have to work extremely hard to reach desired goals. It will take patience and hard work, all done one step at a time.

Soon enough, with adequate training, these players will begin to compete first against their peers and later against other players. Immediately the mental game will prove to be vital. Some will have a different mindset for competitions and will leap forward with their results. Others will face interpersonal challenges such as insecurity, uncertainly, and fears of underperformance. How can two individuals from the same group of people who undergo the same training with the same coaches and training partners develop such significantly different mental states? Seems that training is likely not the cause of the mental deficiencies and these shortcomings come from elsewhere outside of the training facility.

    Dr. Carol Dweck published a great book called "Mindset" explaining two types of mindsets that people generally inhibit – growth mindset and fixed mindset. Growth minded individuals believe that they are capable of learning new things. They are excited to learn and generally thrive in a challenging environment. Fixed mindsets, on the other hand, seem to hit a lot more obstacles in their growth potential because of their beliefs that "they are who they are and cannot change" and that there are some innate predispositions that do not allow them to approach some things differently. Fixed mindsets thrive in an environment when tasks are safely within their capabilities because as Dr. Carol Dweck states, "people with fixed mindset expect ability to show up on its own, before any learning takes place."

    Dr. Carol Dweck offers a lot of insights into how these individuals develop their mindsets. These mindsets form from a very young age and incidentally by exposure to various environments. Some kids begin to value learning above all others and are not afraid to try and fail, while others begin to recognize that status and praise is a lot more valuable and become afraid to fail if they try. The same mindsets are present in table tennis as well.

It is obvious that out of 32 players in a typical tournament event, only one will emerge a champion and it is unreasonable to expect everyone to show immediate results. The initial results, however, are extremely vital to understand the developing player's behavior for the future, especially from the mental mindset perspective. Some will show mediocre results and will be driven to work harder to improve. Some with mediocre results will shut down and face doubt. Some with descent results will be driven to win next time around and also work harder to improve, and some will become satisfied that they reached a certain result deemed "ok" and will instead get a bit cocky and/or lazy. It is only natural. Competition is designed to identify a champion and weeding out all others. Thus, this environment is what sets the tone of first positive or negative emotions and embeds them permanently into the player's behavior and self image. It then becomes extremely important to address any negatives after competition in order to prevent mental gaps that may have settled in player's self-evaluation.

Once several tournaments have been played, the players begin to be seeded based on some kind of a ranking, which again seems to apply pressure on the player. Now, there is a pressure of producing results that are considered norm for the acquired seeding. It seems to be a vicious cycle of never-ending pressure.

Certainly, some matches are a lot more important than others, but the mere fact that the win is not a guarantee or that the match will be incredibly tough sends quite a few players into a state of distress. The first to suffer is the mental game, the second, is the game itself. Before you know it, the very loss that the player was afraid was to happen, happened. All because there is wrong association assigned to a loss. A loss is not a failure! A loss is an indicator of a need for further, harder, and more elaborate training.

The good news is that even the fixed mindsets can change if they truly desire to invest the time and effort into their behavior. Dr. Carol Dweck certainly has a great number of methods on being able to do so. She offers a section of a great quote by a Benjamin Barber, a prominent political theorist, which for this chapter has a lot more value in its entirety.

"I divide the world into learners and non-learners. There are people who learn, who are open to what happens around them, who listen, who hear the lessons. When they do something [unwise], they don't do it again. And when they do something that works a little bit, they do it even better and harder the next time. The question to ask is not whether you are a success or a failure, but whether you are a learner or a non-learner."

If you begin to view match results as an evaluation of training rather than an evaluation of self, you will begin to realize that it is merely a test of improvement. Did my skills improve? Yes, I played a lot better than last time, especially in the following areas. Yet, these areas need more focus in training. The key is learning. If you emerge from the match with at least one new thing you've learned, you have made progress regardless of the result.

My personal mental focus is now reinforced with the same concepts. I started table tennis late in my life and my future in table tennis is not certain. I might not ever have enough time to climb the higher ranks. It's true. However, my biggest rewards are not in titles or trophies. My biggest reward is when someone refers to me as the hardest working player they know. Indeed, it is rewarding to hear those words and these same words and work ethic in turn inspires others.

With this mindset, there is no such thing as failure. As Coach John Wooden of UCLA said "you may be outscored, but you will never lose." Despite of the result, the player succeeds.

Being a champion

There is a very interesting observation that can be made by watching many matches. There are strong players out there that are simply not ready to emerge winners, and then there are weaker players that are prepared to win. The ultimate strength of the mental game is that it can create additional strength that carries a lot more value than the technical aspects of one's game. The best of winning combinations, however, is when a strong player is prepared and ready to be a winner.

This yet again points to the importance of a planned mental preparation. It is not enough to have the skills. The mental game needs to align with player's skills. An improved player needs to act like a champion in order to allow his champion quality game to free flow. Nevertheless, we often find players who go through various intensity of nervousness instilled by a fear of failure, especially when pressured with producing various results. What is the best way to battle the nervousness? How can a player free himself of this impediment?

Nervousness occurs with an uncertainty of a given result and nothing prepares the mental game of the player for the match better than meditation prior to the match. Clearing the mind of useless thoughts that instill doubt and instead replacing them with the thoughts of preparedness. The player has worked extremely hard to play his best game up to this moment and has been fighting to earn his spot for this upcoming challenge. The focus of the meditation is not to project a win as is done in precision sports, but rather a reinforcement of the mental attitude that the player fully deserves an opportunity to play this match. Win or lose, the aim is to put up the best effort forward. The player is not there by accident and is *capable* of winning just as much as the next guy.

This is just an initial preparation. There is more diligence that needs to be taken throughout the match. If jitters occur during the play, a mental intervention is necessary. Clearing of the mind and focusing on the strategy as the way to improve the player's focus is the main method for clearing of the in-game jitters.

If the player takes the steps to prepare before the match and played well throughout the match, and still did not emerge victorious, what was the point you may ask? In this case, I must say, the player lost, but did not fail!

Every player wants to win, but the ones that *only* want to win, are the players most likely to experience failure. These players value only victory. The other players seek evaluation of improvement and learning. They are after knowledge and experience, not the titles of trophies. In the end, the players with a mindset focused on improvement and learning will eventually improve. The players who protect their status will eventually suffer in defeat.

Marlo Thomas published a fantastic two book series titled "The Right Words at the Right Time" which share life experiences and the very words that carried the deepest meaning and the deepest importance for various critical times in people's lives when they really needed to hear thoughts of encouragement and support.

In the second volume of the book, Marlo published stories from the many letters she has received in the mail. Two stories stood out that pertain to this very topic. The first story is about a girl who was struggling with one of her classes in school. Her previous teacher did not accept any mistakes and put so much pressure on her that having advanced to the next grade and getting more difficult assignments was causing her to become extremely distraught and incapable of completing the work. Luckily, the new teacher helped her see a different side of things. The teacher said "we all want everything we do to be perfect, but sometimes it just doesn't turn out that way, because we aren't perfect. If you aren't satisfied when you're done, and you think you can do it better – not perfect, just better, well, then, just do it again. You can do it as many times as you'd like."

The next story that stood out in the book was about a graduate student who decided to go to Japan to experience "Zen life" for her religious education studies. This woman from Kansas spent several days in the monastery assuming a role of a typical in-house nun, following all of the traditions to the finest detail including meals, meditation, and chores. In the end of the second day, completely exhausted and seemingly incapable of continuing tasks required for a nun, she broke down in tears in front of the head nun as she was ironing out monk's robes and was inept in ironing out the robe perfectly. She told the head nun with disappointment,

"I am not doing a good job." The head nun leaned over and said the following words, "… you must remember this. There is no good. And there is no bad. All that matters is how much you try."

These two stories from completely different people in completely different scenarios provide the insight into the proper mental focus necessary for all the tasks. Let's use these profound words to set the proper mental tone of any table tennis player's performance.

There is no such thing in table tennis as an absolute failure, there is no absolute defeat. There is just a chance to learn to do something differently and learn to do it *even* better. Rather than avoiding struggle and seeking an easy way out, being a champion means enjoying, embracing, and striving in face of a difficult challenge and seeking tougher and tougher competition along the way.

Talent

This section is a reflection of my view as a new coach. I believe this topic often comes up in a way to that adds additional unnecessary pressure on the players to perform better and the results, as any results derived under pressure, are a lot more difficult to produce in such environment.

What does it meant to be talented in table tennis? Do you hit harder? Do you spin stronger? Do you always get to the next shot? What skills can be tied to a talent? Is talent measured by results? By level of skills achieved at a young age?

While there are many books and articles on this topic that have been popularized over the years, I believe that talent in table tennis is really not a good measure of a player and should not have any weight in the mental aspects of the game. Unfortunately, the word has a lot of mental associations that seem to provide additional pressure on the players.

Many might argue otherwise, but if talent means innate abilities, the only innate abilities that are present in table tennis are the size of the player (and hence the player's strengths in certain parts of the game possible due to physical characteristic of a player). The speed of learning a given material seems to be innate, but unfortunately because of the individual demands of different players, the numerous different coaching methods that seem to work for most players may not work for some select individuals. It is not truly a "talent" that is missing, but rather a proper training approach that suits the individual learning needs of the player.

Lets take a step back prior to a discovery of Dyslexia, for example. Let's imagine we have two individuals. One with undiagnosed Dyslexia, while another one healthy. Both individuals are taught some material. One picks up things extremely quickly and is considered smart, while another seems to struggle with material and is identified as not smart. Now, we fast forward to our times and we properly diagnose one of the individuals. This person was identified as having difficulties learning, while really the reason learning deficiencies existed were due to an undiagnosed condition. Hence, the general educational process did not work well for an individual with this condition. Yet, when an elaborate teaching curriculum is established specifically to address the needs of an individual with Dyslexia, the condition no longer became an obstacle to learning.[19] All of a sudden, both individuals are equal.

It works the same way with talent. Talent is not achieved. It is perceived with an observer's image by

---

[19] Considering Dr. Carol Dweck's growth mindset, history has shown how many individuals with dyslexia have been able to overcome their obstacles to become successful. Albert Einstein, Leonardo Da Vinci, Thomas Edison, Agatha Christie, Nelson Rockefeller, George Patton, and many others. One of the most famous quotes on overcoming various disabilities came from Winston Churchill regarding his own speech impediment "My impediment is no hindrance." It shows that those who work hard on their impediments are capable of overcoming them.

comparing what the observer sees with his perception of the norms.

Why I am bringing up this topic? Well, simply put, let's change the associations a little bit and provide proper recognition for the players. A player who wins is not any more talented than a player who losses. One player might just work harder, strategize better or has strengths where the opponent has weaknesses. A player who improves is not any more talented than the player who does not. One player might mentally make harder efforts to improve, even though on the outside the player might seem a "natural."

So, when someone says "this player is talented", let's ask more questions. Oh yeah, where does he train? How long has he been training? Who does he train with? How hard does he work out? What are his routines like? What else does he do for training? Read? Does physical exercises? Works with a mental coach?

All of a sudden, the answers to these questions drew a much accurate picture of the player's profile. "This player has the shots, but he has not played long enough to pick up the experience to beat his adversary – that's ok, he is only getting started. Job well done!" No negative associations, no needless pressure to win caused by a label of magical "talent"! The player, however, can be proud of even the smallest achievements. These achievements are simply put, improvements. Players and coaches can certainly take pride in the player's ongoing progress.

Let's evaluate another player – "Oh, that player doesn't train enough anymore." Obviously there should be no disappointment to a loss. His opponent wasn't incredibly "talented" and that is why he beat him, but rather the individual has not been training for some time. No excuses, just a factual statement.

This way, every player's results are reflection of the preparation, work ethics, game strategy, tactics, and stroke execution. In words of Paul Coffey, one of the National Hockey League's legends, "Nobody's a natural. You work hard to get good and then work to get better." This is a true image of the player's skills and capabilities, rather than evaluation of intangible "talents." Why hype up players to set them up for failure. Instead, let's prepare them for competition and set their expectations in a way to directly reflect their current training.

The formula is very simple. The harder one works, the faster that player improves. The improvement, in time, will derive better results.

Intervention

Lots of topics have been covered so far, but I am sure that some readers are thinking "Well, geez, this is all great, but I know I have to concentrate. I know I have to act like a champion to be a champion. I know there is pressure that I need to figure out how to get rid of. But I can't. It's out of my control. What I really need is to learn to play better in a tough situation. How do I get rid of nervous jitters? How do I respond properly to incoming shots? How do I stop freezing? How do I stop missing?"

Before we start evaluating what will allow us to make the shots we are trying to make in a competitive environment, let's first try to understand why we miss and make mistakes. Certainly, poor technique and lack of experience will make us miss, but this is not the type of mistakes this chapter will address. Why do players miss their shots even when their technique and movement have been adequately developed?

If we look at our game, there are several ways we miss our shots. Overdoing it with excessive shots, under doing it by playing safe, and being in a state when we are simply unable to do anything – unable to respond.

The inability to respond is usually solved with improved concentration. Hence, the best way to solve this issue it to find a method that would allow the player to achieve a better state of preparedness. This is usually achieved in training. The training necessary to solve inaction should aim to improve the player's understanding of the rally's shot exchanges, specifically where and when the ball will be most likely returned by the opponent after a given shot. Main focus of such training is to improve anticipation or reduce over anticipation. Knowing when and where to move removes the obstacles of having to figure out an appropriate answer to a given scenario on the fly.

The overdoing or playing safe needs a lot more further analysis as they are in direct relationship with the player's state of mind.

Let's first analyze why some players are playing safe. Yes, it is a result of fear or doubt. Fear of losing a match usually brings out the type of the game the player really does not train to play. Instead of producing the right shots, the player simply contents to controlling the ball.

Seems like a logical solution. If the player does not swing away, the player will likely not miss the shot by overdoing it. However, today's modern game offers a lot of advantages for an attacking player. Passive control against an aggressive, consistent player will probably prove to be effective only for a defensive player whose strategy is to win by attrition. Attacking players do not practice defense as extensively as they train their offensive game. Thus, attackers playing defense will play out of their strengths, which means a less effective game.

There are players that choose to play safe because they simply do not trust their technique. There are all kinds of excuses that come out if asked about the reasons a player decided to play a passive game - "my strokes did not feel good today," "I missed too many shots doing the same thing over and over," and many others. But what is the underlying message of such words? The message they send is simply a lack of trust. Basically, the player does not trust his technique.

When I encounter players not trusting their shots and instead either making up new ones, or playing too passively, or too aggressively, I usually ask these players one question – "Why do we learn technique?" Strangely, there are too many players that do not seem to understand how to answer this question. What is purpose of technique?

Most common response of the players that provide an answer is that we learn technique in order to know how to execute a shot. This moment I usually ask the next question. What does a technically correct shot do? The answer to this question I usually provide myself as some players, the youngsters especially, seem to be a little puzzled with this simple, almost rhetoric question. A technically correct shot will guarantee to place the ball on the table most of the time!

We learn technique in order to know how to consistently and successfully put the ball back on the table in a desired way. Simply put, technique guarantees that the shot will go in most of the time, so there should be no reason to choose another approach as the technical one is statistically a lot more successful. The doubt in the shot making ability is absolutely unfounded when a technical execution is properly developed. The shots executed with proper technique but missed are usually a result of a timing mistake or the result of overdoing it.

The timing issues occur all the time in all levels of the game. Even the best players are not immune to that. Overdoing the shots, on the other hand, is often a result of some mental game deficiency.

Let's look at the reasons the player are exaggerating their shots. Usually this is a player's attempt to drive more power or speed into the ball. At the lower levels, players seem to play "hot potato" when faced with any type of a shot. Players are trying to blast the ball away from them as soon as possible without evaluating proper shot selection. This is usually fixed with improved training, teaching the players to properly time the ball, especially because most players erroneously feel that they do not have enough time to execute a proper stroke. Higher levels, where players have adaptive intelligence and proper technical execution, encounter these types of errors when the players seem to push themselves a bit more in the tactical sense by aiming to take advantage of an opportunity a lot quicker and making an error in judgment of the incoming ball.

Yet, these are far from mental mistakes. These are technical errors. Mental mistakes of overdoing the shot are usually caused by some type of a Napoleon syndrome usually following a great shot. As if the player says to himself: "Oh, yeah? I can hit a great, powerful shot too, I'll show you!" Here comes the ball and... blastoff. Yet another free point awarded to an opponent with an unnecessary shot.

The worst part, however, is that usually big shots missed make most players attempt to execute them again, and often with identical outcome. The players seem to be extremely eager to execute this shot well. They are out to prove it to themselves that they are capable to deliver a big shot. They rush even more and deliver their maximum power. The initial thought of attempting to pull off the big shot and improving confidence by setting up and executing it all over again changes the mental state of the player. Miss first shot, miss another. Before you know it, the curtain opens, enter self-evaluation, and with it, its older brother self-doubt.

Doing too much or too little in shot execution is mostly a symptom of a much bigger mental issue because the player's responses can vary point to point. A player might deal with a shot perfectly in a first shot, drive too much power in next one, and too little power in another one subsequently. This occurs because of the inherent relationship between the points. Under the cover of the match, every player seems to encounter various thoughts of evaluations and assessments of their game. The players constantly try to analyze, explain, and adjust the approach and execution of their shots. Yet, not all of the evaluations are the same and it is extremely important to understand what type of analysis is mentally sound as there are some evaluations that are extremely detrimental to player's performance.

Imagine yourself executing a shot and missing it, what is the typical next thought that goes through your head? Most players do not realize that they are projecting negative thoughts frequently by correcting their techniques with statements such as "Don't do this, and don't do that." What happens when you instruct yourself something by stating "don't?" Somehow magically you will do exactly what you have tried not to do. This is because the negative association of the word "don't" injects preventive action and focuses our attention on it, rather than focusing the attention on a corrective action. This principle is even more imperative when a player is receiving coaching instruction. If the coach says "don't do that," an unwary player simply follows the instruction to avoid making an action, instead of being guided by an instruction on what exactly should be done.

However, adjustments get even more complicated. Let's void the word "don't" and state adjustments in a positive way. "Ok, you not moving fast enough, need to get there faster." Next rally plays out, we think "Ok, better, but now you're too fast, slow it down." Next shot, "Ok, now look at the ball, close the angle for topspin." Then, on the next point, we seem to identify yet another area of the stroke or technique that needs to be corrected.

It is certainly natural to think about the adjustments being made, but unfortunately when we begin to adjust in micro movements, we begin to open the room for evaluations. "This shot is bad." "That shot is no good." "What a horrific forehand." "You're too slow." "I can't believe I missed this shot." While the thoughts of adjustments are ok, the problem is that the evaluations assign a value to the mistakes and turn them into judgments, which have a severe impact on the player's performance.

Brad Gilbert provided a very good insight into breaking down opponent's mental state by dismantling a player's trust of his confidence shot. He made an observation that in tennis, a forehand is the main shot of every player and if a player begins to miss his strongest and most consistent shot, then he will begin to fall apart mentally. Therefore, forehand in tennis is the ultimate confidence shot. As long forehand seems to produce results, the player's mental game remains intact, but when the mistakes start numbering, the player's mental state drifts into abyss. Hence, Brad's game was built around the aspect of unnerving the mental state of the player through a vast variety of shots played into opponent's strength. His purpose was to force the opponent to begin thinking about his shots and begin to introduce doubt by mind's automatic ability to judge and assign value to each of the shots. If the player's strongest shots don't work, how can that player expect to win?

How does mental judgment works and why is this type of judgment destructive? In his book "The inner game of tennis," Timothy Gallwey describes this judgment as "the act of assigning a negative or positive value to the event." In his words, judgment is saying that "some events within your experience are good and you like them, and other events in your experience are bad and you don't like them. You don't like the sight of yourself hitting the ball into the net, but you judge as good the sight of your opponent being aced by your serve. Thus, judgments are our personal, ego reactions to the sights, sounds, feelings and thoughts within our experience."

Timothy Gallwey points out that judgment described above provokes the thinking process that inevitably begins to engage the conscious mind to perform many movements, while the evaluations continue. In due time, our mind begins to take shortcuts and group evaluations into a set of related, generalized events. A single typical mistake in stroke mechanics will eventually turn into a thought of "Oh, not again, you keep missing that shot." Even when a player is happy with his shots, there is a false sense of security since it is "impossible to judge some events as positive without judging other events as negative."

Slowly but surely, the innocent proactive thoughts of adjustment to a ball that have real purpose and need within the match have set a mental trap that so many players seem to fall into. These types of evaluations, especially after the mind connects them into generalized symptomatic problem, just force the player to "try" to make the shots, inevitably controlling their body with conscious mind. Thus, the players enter the so called "learning mode." The players begin to try to come up with strokes by varying their approaches and testing the waters as it is done in training. But, in training, missing is part of learning. In competition, missing means losing.

Let's recall a training session where the emphasis is on learning or improving it. First thing the player does is begin to supply more power into the stroke. The pressure to make every single shot is absent, so the strokes flow freely and oddly are very consistent. With much emphasis on training reflecting a real competitive environment of playing within the balance of maximum power and maximum control, the learning mode feels that the player is able to achieve best result with maximum power input. However, in a real match, the approach with maximum force results in a lot of shots missed by slightly overdoing it.

The players should be relying on the prior training to have a known and predetermined response already "recorded" in subconscious mind. Many players feel awkward during the matches because they are unable to allow their subconscious "autopilot" mode to engage and still force their bodies to perform movements from manual instructions. No wonder players get nervous in their matches, they simply do not know what to expect from themselves. One moment they are dead on with their shots and are on fire and the next moment, the same person can't put even the easiest shot on the table.

Some players make a claim that table tennis is a game of streaks. The players seem to be able to score points in succession and usually the player with the best ability to continue streaks will emerge victorious. I don't quite agree that table tennis is a game of streaks. Rather, it is a game of concentration and mental focus. The player capable of retaining the focus without interruptions by staying clear of evaluations and other distractions, by staying calm and attentive in any point regardless of the score on the board will be much more likely to win the match. Without adequate focus, however, the player's ability to secure the points will fluctuate depending on the actual mental state of the player point to point. If a player is ready and focused, he will be capable of scoring the points, if he is not, he will likely lose them quite easily.

How often have you seen someone being ahead by a large number of points, but losing? Did this player's streak just end? I think statistically it is very improbable that something like this would happen as frequently as it occurs in table tennis. Some players concentrate well to create leads. They play smooth, without prior expectations. They do not judge themselves and do not overdo their shots. Then, all of a sudden, they feel a sense of superiority. They feel like they are in a "zone." However, as soon as the player achieves some kind of affirmation of their performance in a "zone", this player begins to falter. Timothy Gallwey points out to the delusion of such magical "zone." "The 'hot streak' usually continues until he starts thinking about it and tries to maintain it; as soon as he attempts to exercise control, he loses it."

So what is the proper solution to the optimal player's performance? How does one achieve the best state of mind to be able to compete with the best game possible?

Obviously first goal is to learn to play without assumptions – to take the game one point at a time, whether in a lead or in a deficit. Any extra pressure added due to the current score will only pull the player back into the state of doubt.

On mistakes and errors, it is important to stay clear of dwelling on the previous point. Note the cause of a mistake, but instead of making many manual adjustments by analyzing all of the moving parts during stroke execution and adjusting each of the moving parts one at a time, simply recall the right way it should be done. The aim here is to allow the subconscious mind to come up with proper execution automatically.

The other alternative is to think placement above stoke mechanics. This way subconscious mind will automatically find the way to produce a desired shot. The only thing for which the conscious mind needs to be called upon is to remember the *feeling* of what the proper execution of the shot feels like.

Close your eyes for a moment and think of a shot you've done in the past. Try to remember how it felt hitting a certain ball. Now, repeat and see if it works. A known, familiar feeling will automatically bring back the proper execution of the shot and with it, recover the confidence needed for a competitive environment.

I know how it sounds, a bit too magical to be true. When I first encountered this advice in Timothy Gallwey's book, I was quite skeptical, yet having tested it, I believe it is relatively easy to adopt into every player's skill set. Instead of trying to use the conscious mind in reiterating each part of the stroke in a sequence, recall the feeling of producing a desired shot in the past. Once the feeling of the shot is recalled, the body will repeat it automatically.

Finally, put your faith in your skills, your training, and your technique. It's okay to miss. Everyone does. But, it is okay to miss only when playing *your* game and executing the shots you have developed in training. Any improvisations or half commits usually produce an opposite result. A mental approach based on trust, on the other hand, relaxes the muscles, improves concentration, and allows the game to play out naturally and freely with much improved results in the end.

Knowing self

Every individual has certain unique predispositions in pretty much everything around. As we grow from child to adult and mature, we all go through different experiences in our lives and each one of us develops a different understanding and a point of view on various topics. With strong influences from the past, we derive and adopt a different set of values, which guide the rest of our lives. When it comes to sports, these experiences have a significant and direct impact on the way we think, act, and solve problems in a competitive environment as well because, as Heywood Broun quoted, "Sports do not build character. They reveal it."

Table tennis skills are fairly easy to develop in comparison with player's ability to formulate a sound mental game. This is one of the reasons why it takes such a long time for an average player to mature from beginner and intermediate levels to advanced, and farther up from advanced to semi-pro and pro. In this regard, it makes sense for each player to invest time into learning more about self and making use of the gathered knowledge to develop a solid mental game. Without a solid mental game, even the best players can slip into their predisposed mental zones and can develop numerous negative behaviors preventing further progress forward.

If we begin to analyze ourselves in more detail, we find that there is something in our cognitive behavior makes us respond in a predisposed unique way to similar situations. Most of us, however, do not take a step back to discover where these mental predispositions originated and how we can change them, especially if they are impeding our ability to fulfill all of our potential in a competitive environment.

There are a lot of various behaviors that players seem to reveal during competitions that hampers player's ultimate growth, but among them are a few very common ones.

First view is that excessive self-criticism, which comes out in very negative tones. Second, is what I'd like to call a weaker player syndrome where the player is constantly in a mode resembling a fight for his life to prove that he is not worse than his adversary. Then, there are players who try their best, but give up with even a little bit of consistent resistance or lose interest in an environment lacking challenge. The attitude of such players is "I'll try to do it, but if I can't or it's too boring, oh well." There are also players that tend to work extremely hard, but rarely if ever enter competition since they "are not ready." Year after year, such players train without evaluating their true potential. Finally, there are some players that purposefully do not try to succeed. Their view is that with success, they will get even more pressure. Failure to succeed, however, lets them remain in a status quo where their self-image is safely kept intact. These are usually disinterested players forced to stay in the game for one reason or another.

Most of these players, however, have one thing in common. They all seem to be stuck in a fixed mindset where their beliefs are that they are the way they are and that they simply cannot change. These beliefs are reinforced by the fact that they have tried to improve many times and all without significant success. For these players things seem hopeless. The rational seems logical. Fortunately for them, his point of view is absolutely flawed.

It is very hard to change individual whole and complete self-image. It is practically impossible to change everything, especially all at once either, but every individual can change one small thing at a time.

For example, some people who attempt to quit smoking try to immediately drop the cigarettes on day X, and promise to halt smoking from that moment on. Rarely does this work. People have been more successful in quitting it by a slow paced phase out approach by smoking less every month, week, and day until they are completely smoke free. But these plans have one similar issue, they all retain the mental focus on the actual act of smoking and simply try to do it less, while in reality there is another approach that is a lot more simple and successful in the long term.

If the person asks him or herself why they really smoke and start analyzing when they have the urge to smoke, they will discover that smoking is an activity instilled into the daily routine as a substitute of another action. At work, smoke is synonymous with break time. During the party, it stands for conversing. At home, for someone with a rowdy family it stands for a need to escape the chaos, for someone with a quiet house, it stands for needing to step outside and seeing the people or nature. For someone who is busy working, it is used as a tool to achieve concentration.

Smoking is really a poor substitute to a certain action and if that is the case, then the best way to break this habit is to substitute the action of smoking with another action. While scientists may argue that nicotine withdrawal actually exists and that there is a pharmacological effect of the drug on a human being that will prevent someone from being able to quit, what would explain the fact that there are people who quit easily without intervention of drugs and therapists while others do not? Again, scientists will argue that some people are more biologically predisposed than others, but it can also be argued that it's not biological, but rather that every person has a different strength of will. This is the crossroad where the mindsets again will collide. Fixed mindsets, described by Carol Dweck, will argue that they cannot change and are controlled by the substance, but growth minded individuals will approach the dilemma by learning many ways to help them break the habit. In the long run, it doesn't matter what kind of means are available for each individual. What is important is that change is possible for everyone.

Now let's go back to table tennis. Can the players with negative mental traits change? I am convinced that the answer is yes. This does not mean that every player will be a winner, but it will allow someone to lift their limitations a notch higher, which for some players is an achievement equating to fulfilling their dream.

How does a player facilitate this change? First and foremost, leave out the pessimism and doubt. Everyone has doubt, but some players can shield themselves from it, while others seem to be conquered by it. The reason is that doubt creates uncertainty. But, why concentrate on an uncertainty when there is something definite and guaranteed for every player in every match?

I'm sure that most can remember coming home after school when they were younger and the parents asked them a very simple question "What did you learn in school today?" While some kids preferred to ignore the question with a quick answer of "nothing", in reality every kid had an *opportunity* to learn *something*. And this is the guarantee for every student of every discipline. In table tennis, every player receives this guarantee.

With a mental focus set on learning, the pressure, negative thoughts, feelings, and doubts no longer assume a dominant position. The doors are now open to improvement. The players with negative traits can certainly benefit from this type of a mental focus. What about the players with a mental issue of trying to constantly prove themselves worthy?

The need to prove oneself is usually derived from childhood where an individual was constantly subjected to other's evaluations of size, strength, speed, or maybe smarts. This person was always unsoundly or maybe too protectively described as "too small to do this, too weak to do that, too sick to participate." As the person grows up, these types of emotions remain almost permanently embedded in the player's minds. Individuals that convert such experiences into energy for relentless hard work usually do not encounter drastic impediments in their development as long as their goals are farsighted. However, the players that need immediate and frequent recognition of their worthiness every step of their development suffer significant setbacks. These players seem to play the game with excessive aggression. They approach the game with rage. As if the player is Mike Tyson getting ready to enter the ring with Lennox Lewis, the player is speaking Mike Tyson's words with his strokes - "I want to rip out his heart and feed it to him. I want to kill people. I want to rip their stomachs out and eat their children." Before you know it, the players get used to always going for big shots. If they go slow, they miss, so there is just no other way to approach their shots. No wonder, this type of a game is a suicide mission more often than not. No wonder the mental game remains angrier. The shots get faster, harder, and more powerful. But... they rarely hit the table.

These players can certainly benefit from a lesson in history. The most famous and oldest competitions that are embraced and highly valued to this day are the Olympic Games. The purpose of the competition was a benevolent one. Greek cities idealized physical abilities and discipline. The goal of the games was to demonstrate the physical strengths of participants from different cities and show off their capabilities in a public format. All sports were conducted in spirit of *honorable competition* and winners became immediate home town heroes.

Given that the Greek cities competing against one another frequently waged deadly wars against each other as well, the games were a way to achieve a temporary truth. The desire of the games was not to fight to the death. Certainly wresting and boxing events were rough, but that is simply the nature of contact sports. The spirit of competition was to show off and celebrate athletes of best abilities. The essence of the games was *peaceful rivalry*.

For table tennis players that seem to be overcome with rage and anger, it is important to realize that competition is synonymous with challenge. The challenge is simply a test of your skills, only in this test, there are no grades. The test is there to measure progress and the best way to measure progress is to compare it with other similarly improvement oriented players. Opponent is not a deadly enemy. Opponent is your test collaborator. The test will show what improved a lot, what improved a little, and what needs more work to improve.

Now let's look at the last set of players. These players are full of excuses and seem to hide behind them every step of the way. Skill wise, these players are the cream of the crop, but where they fall way below the norm is in motivation.

Motivation is the energy that drives the player to work hard towards their goals, but motivation has its own source of energy – desire! It is important to have desire to achieve even a smallest goal. Yet, a common mistake players make is that they pick a goal that is way beyond their reach.

Let's recall an example from chess. Grandmasters can find ideal placement of their pieces and they can count the moves backwards to identify the steps they need to take to assume a desired position. This makes the plan simple, but let's put the pieces into starting position and then clear out the board altogether and put a checkmate on the board in a particular way. Even the best grandmasters in the world won't guarantee that they will reach that checkmate position because there are almost an infinite number of moves that remain between the current position and the original one. With so many moves uncertain, how can someone plan? How can someone know the steps that need to be taken? How can someone project when the plan might finally come to fruition?

Without a plan, the player is unable to evaluate the progress. Without evaluating progress, the player cannot determine the priority of things that need attention in training. Without training aimed to work on the most important weakness of the game, the player produces the same results. Without any further detail, there is no clear idea when the player will improve. The cycle is vicious and the progress remains unseen. Finally, without progress, motivation dissipates and the excuses roll out as the last ditch effort to protect the individuals' self-confidence.

Excuses are quite contagious. One excuse brings out the other, and the next, and then the next. The only way to stop it is to halt and re-plan. What does it mean to plan properly? It means aiming to reach small, reasonable, and attainable goals. Fortunately for the players, there is a way to recuperate from a lack of motivation. Reaching even the smallest goals achieves a little bit of confidence. With more confidence, reaching the next goal is easier and will derive even more desire to draft and work towards the next goal. Success is extremely addictive and as the old saying goes "if there is a will, there is a way."

    Brad Gilbert described Andre Agassi's struggle with his game after a wrist injury in his book. It looked like Andre's career was coming to a grinding halt. He had poor mental state and couldn't find a way to beat even the "easiest" players on the Pro Tour. Everything in his matches seemed to go wrong. This is when Brad gave him a very simple advice to play in Challenger Series tournaments designed for players ranked below world's top 50. The aim was to put him in an environment where he could complete and win despite his weakened mental state and fear of reoccurring injury. Andre was reluctant at first, but listened, participated, and won. This was a beginning of a new revival. Andre won many titles since that year, including becoming at the time only the fifth male player to win all four Grand Slam singles titles. His achievements were possible because his confidence was restored.

    So what does it mean to know "thyself"? A player who knows himself is constantly observing and evaluating his actions against his mental inclinations. To know the mental inclinations, however, the player constantly immerses himself into a state of learning – learning about himself, his behaviors, his tendencies, his highs and lows, and ups and downs. It means to be honest with your real strengths and weaknesses – acknowledging improvements and shortcomings alike. It is not a single analysis. It is an ongoing long term commitment. It is a method of constant discovery and refinement because, and I emphasize this again, with a learning mentality, there will be improvement and there will be growth in many things even beyond table tennis.

Dan Seemiller said the following great words: "Excellence may be harder to achieve when one is focused on trying to achieve it. If you wish to be at your best as often as possible, focus on being focused, not on winning or peer approval."

It's not possible to force the improvement, but it is possible and important to facilitate it by combining the work ethic and the mental focus into a single unified plan. The player will still not know when the improvement will come, but one day, it will just happen. The hardest task will be to stay on course.

The Next Step

"I am building a fire, and everyday I train, I add more fuel. At just the right moment, I light the match."

- Mia Hamm

Table tennis is a very complex sport not only because it is considered one of the fastest sports in the world. It is complex because in addition to complexities within techniques, tactics, strategy, and mental game, there is also a very strong relationship between them. This relationship explains the reason why some players stagnate and others improve, why some players reach higher levels, while others do not.

The relationship between various parts of the game develops from the moment the person is first exposed to the game. Players who start out this game first learn a few basic shots. Then, they learn to put these shots to use. Finally, they figure out how to manipulate the opponent to score their points. This is usually the basic road map of a hobby player.

Hobby players begin their journey with some kind of a technique, no matter how good or bad it may be, and then they learn to use their shots to score points. A few shots mixed with basic tactics is usually enough to build a competitive recreational game. Hobby player does not focus or even care about a strategic or mental dimension of the game yet. This type of a player plays for fun without expectations. Nerves or farsighted strategic thoughts are simply unnecessary for mere enjoyment of the activity, yet this picture changes drastically as the player decides to play this game a little bit more seriously.

The learning process evolves. At the forefront of the learning process is a desire to develop stronger shots. However, the strongest shots need a proper technique. Hence, learning converges on a need to learn a proper technique. Once the strokes improve, the player is exposed to the tactical game by learning to combine shots into combinations.

Now, the player is at a crossroad. The choice is simple and yet, leads to very different paths. If the player enters competition, the player will likely discover the need for a development of a mental game and may decide to improve it. On the other hand, the player could likely continue working on the technical skills. Some players at this juncture will decide to develop stronger tactics and some very few aim to improve their strategy. Yet, each path from now on is different and comes with its own set of challenges. This is what it means to take the next step. It means identify the next element of the game that needs to be further improved.

Therefore, the balance of skills for every player is never the same in all aspects of the game. Players that develop solid techniques early will need to catch up their tactical and strategic thinking along with the mental game to solidify their performance. Even the strongest technical players will eventually need to even out the skill level of other parts of the game. Until then, the game will likely be up and down.

Some players work on the strategic and tactical game a lot sooner. They don't have beautiful strokes, but they figure out how to minimize opponent's strengths and maximize their own. These players usually build up a much stronger mental game and can frequently defeat much technically stronger opponents. However, these players also find that over time, they will eventually reach the ceiling based on their technical limitations. Strategic, tactical, and mental strength will be neutralized by the stronger and more consistent opponents.

Still, there are numerous types of players. There are players with great tactics, but without adequate strategy, players with excellent techniques, tactics and strategy, but without a solid mental focus, and many more. All of these players need to even out all parts of their game to progress forward. The improvement, therefore, is not a final state, but merely a cycle.

The learning cycle does not always happen within a training environment. Improvement occurs in two ways - with deliberate training and incidentally through experience. In addition to dedicated training, players can progress their game automatically simply by playing matches. As a matter of fact, most improvement happens spontaneously and seamlessly. One day the player plays like the old self, and another day seems to have taken a significant jump. The fact is that every player's game constantly evolves in many subtle ways. Sometimes so subtle, that even the players and their coaches do not immediately recognize the changes. These are basics of the inherent complexity of the sport and its relationship between the many "moving parts" of the game.

The reason why some players find it difficult to improve and others do not depends on the gaps that exist within every player's game. Fast improving players find their skills evolving so fast that the other parts of their game are unable to catch up. Stable players who seem to found an ideal way to play their game reach an ultimate technical limitation of their game impeding their further progress. Then, there are players whose games seamlessly evolved into a less effective form simply by playing for fun without any specific goals.

Imagine a strong player without a good strategy, for example, a player who has an excellent serve and a 3rd ball attack. This player will find success until his level goes up far enough where opponents' service return and defense is strong enough to prevent the player from gaining a significant advantage. This player will begin to stagnate at this level until the rest of the developmental weaknesses are closed up.

Now let's look at another common stereotype – player with excellent mental and strategic game, but clearly weaker technical strengths. This player might be successful defeating opponents up to a certain level based only on a superior strategic and mental game, but once this player will advance to play higher skilled opponents, the player will stagnate until his technical skills develop to withstand higher level shots.

Frequently the explanation for lack of improvement is hidden behind a mystical phrase that "table tennis is a game of style," and that the player simply struggles against a given style. However, if we look deeper at the challenges the player faces during the match against a player whose "style" is difficult to overcome, it is not the style that is to blame, but rather player's technical limitations do not allow the player to properly respond to shots produced by his opponent.

A complete balance of skills in all parts of the game facilitates steady and consistent development. When a relatively even balance of skills in technique, tactics, strategy, and the mental game is achieved, even though it is not clear when the improvement will happen, the player is ready to take the next jump. When the jump finally occurs, the player and/or the coach will need to decide on the next skill to learn or improve. And yet again the question arises. Should the player start the next step to improvement by advancing his technique, strategy, tactics, or the mental game?

Obviously, everything depends on the technical abilities of the player. How can one expect to follow a winning strategy or tactic if the player is unable to execute the type of a shot necessary for the strategy? Even with a positive mental focus and a good mental preparation and attitude, the player cannot force himself to consistently deliver a high quality desired shot if the player does not have the technical foundation to execute such a shot.

Let's play a variation of a fantasy table tennis by imagining a player with skills in various parts of the game. We can come up with a lot of types of players. For example, a tactically strong player with a good technical foundation who can mount strong offensive attacks and emerge victorious. But if such player has a weak mental game, his task would be a lot harder to achieve. This player will likely also struggle against a consistent opponent who can find and expose a strategic weakness. Yet, combine this tactically strong player with a good mental game and an opponent with an excellent technique but a weaker mental game and you have a recipe for success. In this combination, it seems that a player with strong tactics, sound technique, and good mental game will be successful against most opponents. Yet, if we were to create a match up opponent to withstand this player, we can envision producing someone with a sound strategic game that would limit the player's tactical strengths and also a good mental game that would withstand the pressure created by vicious tactics.

Fantasy table tennis can be played in many ways by imagining players with strengths and weaknesses in many areas, as the combinations are quite numerous. However, from the learning progress perspective, there are some inherent strategic weaknesses that can be recognized among many of the real players. Most common strategic mistake is progressing one part of the game several levels up from the other parts of the game.

Imbalance of skills is the main element separating the good players from the great players. Good players are the ones who figure out how to utilize their existing skills to improve, but great players are the ones that learn the skills necessary to improve the game. The good news is that the steps for improvement for every player are fairly easy to identify.

The first step is to figure out the current state of the player's game. Are there any gaps that need to be fulfilled to reach a relative balance in technique, tactics, strategy, and mental game? If the answer is yes, then the first goal is to achieve balance. Then, the next step would be to progress technique a step forward – to play with better speed, placement, and spin. Then, the next step is to progress the tactics and strategy to match the technical strength. Finally, the cycle ends with mental reinforcement allowing the player to use the full technical abilities, tactics, and strategy under a pressure of a match.

If you, the reader, are a table tennis player, what's your next step? Whether you know the answer already, or whether you are seeking some advice, the prior sections of the book will hint the way.

Conclusion

"The discipline of writing something down is the first step toward making it happen."

-- Lee Iacocca

When I drafted the first pages of this book, I immediately knew that I took on an incredibly ambitious task by aiming to describe so many areas of a table tennis game. Many different kinds of relationships among the many elements of table tennis led me to often cover the same topic from a slightly different perspective. At times it looked like a repeat of the material that has already been described. Yet, it was intentional. And even now, after having gone through the review of the book, every time I re-read a given topic, more thoughts emerge. With the last chapters marked as complete, I find that there are still many places to expand upon in the future.

As you can see, there is no shortage of material to cover because, unfortunately, or perhaps fortunately in my case, the prior generations of players and coaches have been scarce in sharing some of the information in a written form. Certainly, it is understood. Table tennis is a game where knowledge is power. Yet, there are a lot more resources available to everyone other than books. The development of the video capturing and sharing that seems to catch various training routines and exercises along with matches provides a good insight into the state of the sport today and its future in years to come. My aim, however, is to continue trying to fulfill the void of information for further development of the sport, so that elite ranks are not just dreams for certain few, but viable possibilities for many types of players.

I hope this book becomes yet another asset for a player aiming to achieve new heights of the game, to break plateaus, and to progress to higher ranks. As Russell Simmons said "If you learn late, you pass it on to people so that they can learn it early." Indeed, I started playing table tennis late, but I look forward to the shared knowledge being useful for other players in every intended way.

June 30, 2013

Contributors

I would like to extend a special thank you to two-time U.S. Table Tennis Olympian Sean O'Neill and a team of table tennis enthusiasts from MyTableTennis.Net forum for reviewing the original book manuscript and providing invaluable feedback:

Baal

Beeray1

Fatt

Haggisv

Imago

Mhnh007

Rahul_TT

Ripag

Roundrobin

Slevin

Speedplay

ZApenholder

Another special thank you goes to Zoran Stefanovski for taking ideas for a book cover and bringing them to life.

References

- "Train to Win" by Michel Gadal
- "Winning Ugly" by Brad Gilbert
- "I've Got Your Back" by Brad Gilbert
- "Bounce" by Matthew Syed
- "Talent is Overrated" by Geoff Colvin
- "Mindset" Dr. Carol Dweck
- "The Right Words at the Right Time. Volume 2: Your Turn" by Marlo Thomas
- "Think to Win" by Allen Fox
- "The Inner Game of Tennis" by Timothy Gallway
- "Winning Table Tennis: Skills, Drills, and Strategies" by Daniel Seemiller & Mark Hollowchak
- "With Winning in Mind" by Lenny Bassham
- "Table Tennis: Skills, Techniques, Tactics" by Jenny Heaton

Made in the USA
Columbia, SC
07 February 2019